WHAT PEOPLE ARE SAYING ABOUT

DANIEL DEFOE AND
THE BANK OF ENGLAND

This is an engaging and distinctive book about the links between the history of the novel and the Bank of England. Hamilton and Parker's work is an original contribution to our growing critical understanding of the fictional dimensions of finance and financial institutions.

Professor Nicholas Royle, Literature, University of Sussex

A bold and exciting fusion of literary and financial history, this provocative organisational study takes us to the very heart of the modern.

David Kynaston, author and social historian

Though whisper it quietly, much of research in business would bore the bum off a buffalo. This on the other hand is an interdisciplinary masterpiece standing between English Literature and Management which is an exciting tale of risk, danger, piratical endeavour, plunder, deceit and daring-do in the Age of Projects. It is a beautifully realised narrative interweaving the rise of the Bank of England with the economy of Scotland, Daniel Defoe's biography and the story of Moll Flanders. It provides literary enjoyment and real insight into the contemporary world in equal measure. It's a treasure.

Professor Gibson Burrell, Management, University of Leicester

Daniel Defoe and the Bank of England

The Dark Arts of Projectors

Daniel Defoe and the Bank of England

The Dark Arts of Projectors

Valerie Hamilton and Martin Parker

zero
books

Winchester, UK
Washington, USA

First published by Zero Books, 2016
Zero Books is an imprint of John Hunt Publishing Ltd., Laurel House, Station Approach,
Alresford, Hants, SO24 9JH, UK
office1@jhpbooks.net
www.johnhuntpublishing.com
www.zero-books.net

For distributor details and how to order please visit the 'Ordering' section on our website.

Text copyright: Valerie Hamilton and Martin Parker 2015

ISBN: 978 1 78279 952 8
Library of Congress Control Number: 2015946046

A CIP catalogue record for this book is available from the British Library.

Design: Lee Nash

Printed and bound by CPI Group (UK) Ltd, Croydon, CR0 4YY, UK

We operate a distinctive and ethical publishing philosophy in all
areas of our business, from our global network of authors to
production and worldwide distribution.

CONTENTS

'as is not seldom the case with projectors, by insensible gradations proceeding from comparatively pigmy aims to titanic ones, the original scheme had, in its anticipated eventualities, at last attained to an unheard-of degree of daring.'

(Herman Melville, 'The Bell-Tower', 1855)

Acknowledgements

The following people have read all or part of this book at various stages of its growth. We very much appreciate their comments.

Chris Piper, Business Support Unit, Bank of England; Mark Robson, Statistics, Bank of England; John Footman, Central Services, Bank of England; John Keyworth, Curator, Bank of England; Malcolm Hamilton, Project Director, KEO Construction; Chris Davies, Compliance, Societé Generale; Matthew Mortimer, Director, AMP; Chris Perkins, Investment, Prudential Property Management; Martin Moore, Investment, Prudential Property Management; Ann Halpern, HR, Norton Rose International Law Firm; Carolann Edwards, HR, Norton Rose International Law Firm; Margot Shilling, Marketing, PPP; Vincent Quinn, Nicholas Royle and Norman Vance, University of Sussex; Gibson Burrell, Valerie Fournier and David Harvie, University of Leicester; Fiona Anderson-Gough, University of Warwick; Dorothea Noble, University of Hertfordshire; Peter Fraser, University of Hertfordshire; Penny Pritchard: University of Hertfordshire; Bookclub (Belinda, Di, Kate, Sue, Angela, Debbie, Dawn, Jacqui, Jo); and Charlotte and Helen Mortimer.

1

Novels, and Banks, and Disciplines

'In weakness we create distinctions, then
Believe that all our puny boundaries are things
Which we perceive and not which we have made.'
(William Wordsworth, c.1799[1])

Projects and projecting

A novel and an organization would generally be regarded as unrelated things, members of different categories. One deals in airy matters of fiction, the other in brute economic realities. This book explores the proposition that the novel and the organization share fundamental characteristics of form, function and technique. That is to say, they work in the same way. We explore this idea by comparing the emergence of an early English novel by Daniel Defoe, *Moll Flanders* (1722), and an early English corporation, the Bank of England (1694). It seems to us that the period from which they emerged, sometimes called the 'Age of Projects' (1680–1720), is inherent in, and inherited by, the form of the novel and the corporation respectively. They are projects of a projecting age. The metaphor of the 'project', the risky adventure, is taken from Defoe's *Essay upon Projects* (1697) and is used as a lens through which to reveal the entangled relationship between the novel and the corporation. The eighteenth-century 'projector' would now be called an 'entrepreneur'; but in the eighteenth century the figure had not yet gained the mythological proportions which it attains in the late twentieth century. The darker side of the projector was well recognized. This was someone who was admired and feared. A schemer who engaged in fantastic speculation in order to convince others to invest in their imaginings, to give them credit and therefore substance.

1

Fiction and fact relied on each other then, and it seems to us that the lesson of this book is that they still do.

Now we aren't the first people to enter this territory. There is a respected body of literary criticism and cultural history that establishes connections between the eighteenth-century novel, finance, and capitalism[2], and we build on these insights. However, our specific focus on the organization, the corporation, allows us to compare the beginnings of two institutions that have shaped the modern world. Significantly, we try to avoid taking too academic an approach and instead enact or reconstitute the interdisciplinary relationship between fact and fiction in the telling of this tale. So, dear reader, don't only approach this as a history lesson about the beginnings of contemporary capitalism, but also a confabulation about the relationship between fact and fiction. The very idea of there being separate domains of culture and of economy is challenged by the story we will tell. As the Canadian cultural studies academic Max Haiven puts it, Marx's term 'fictitious capital' is more than an offhand dismissal of something he doesn't like, but can also be understood as a description of the ontology of capitalism itself. Money is made with fiction and narrative, just as fictions and narratives can be sold for money.[3]

This relationship is belied by the gulfs of incomprehension that currently divide university Literature departments from Business schools. We want our readers to think about and challenge this division that assumes a matter-of-fact solidity to organizations whilst approaching novels as if they were mere commentary. This is an interdisciplinary book, in the sense that it lies between categories that are normally assumed to be discreet, comprehensible and solid. We want to show that they are actually rather dubious, puny boundaries that we have made, not things that are there in the world. Most importantly, this is a good story. A tale of risk, danger, pirates, treasure, deceit and daring-do. It's a tale we want people to read, enjoy and marvel at. The discerning reader, and of course that's you, might want to repeat parts of this tale to friends and colleagues, and the uncanny elements of our story will doubtless stir a sense of there being strange, accidental inevitabilities in all our lives.

Most of our tale is set at the close of the seventeenth century and the beginning of the eighteenth: a period of extreme inventiveness. The figure of Daniel Defoe, inventor, businessman, writer, politician and secret agent, characterizes the age. His first published work, *An Essay upon Projects* (1697), bottles this energy. It is a series of proposals for the social and economic improvement of the nation – on banks, lotteries, seamen, women's education and many other topics. Defoe explains that the richness of ideas at this time was generated from 'the humour of invention', which produced 'new contrivances, engines, and projects to get money'. One of the keenest and most thriving areas of invention was the emerging joint-stock companies. Colin Nicholson in *Writing and Finance* observes that there was a veritable 'rash' of projects in the early 1690s and that in the period preceding the collapse of the South Sea Company in 1720, '200 insurance companies were floated in London alone'.[4] The economic historian, Sir John Clapham, reports that in 1692 'there had not been twenty companies in Britain', but by 1695 there were at least 150.[5]

Defoe seems to have coined the term 'The Projecting Age'. He is characteristically astute in his attempt to define a project as understood at this time:

> The building of Babel was a right project; for indeed the true definition of a project, according to modern acceptation, is, as is said before, a vast undertaking, too big to be managed, and therefore likely to come to nothing.[6]

The 'essential ends of a project', he declares, in anticipation of Adam Smith's economic philosophy some seventy years later, are that it should attempt to fulfil 'public and private want'. A project requires good providence, he argues, for some projects, although wildly unlikely, do succeed. He gives the example of William Phips' project to search for sunken Spanish treasure, a project that, we reveal later, proves central to the story of the Bank of England.

> Witness Sir William Phips' voyage to the wreck; it was a mere project; a lottery of a hundred thousand to one odds; a hazard which, had it failed, everybody would have been ashamed to have owned themselves concerned in; a voyage that would have been as much ridiculed as Don Quixote's adventure upon the windmill. Bless us! That folks should go three thousand miles to angle in the open sea for pieces of eight! Why, they should have made ballads of it, and the merchants would have said of every unlikely adventure, "It was like Phips's wreck-voyage." But it had success and who reflects upon the project?[7]

Defoe himself here compares a project to a story. Phips' risky venture is compared to the one undertaken by Don Quixote, the 1605 chivalric adventure that is a contender for the honor of being recognized as the first novel. Both Cervantes and Phips were speculators, Defoe suggests. They initiated projects that could have been part of the litter of history, but ended up having ramifications way beyond their projector's expectations.

Defoe is clear that a project is judged, in the end, by whether it succeeds, not by whether it was a sensible bet:

> Endeavour bears a value more or less,
> Just as 'tis recommended by success:
> The lucky coxcomb every man will prize,
> And prosp'rous actions always pass for wise.[8]

Some projects are hazardous and deceptively presented; 'And yet success has so sanctified' some 'that it would be a kind of blasphemy against fortune to disallow them'. 'Blasphemy' introduces a religious element to fortune, as a power that is beyond the influence of mere mortals. A project, in the end, is always subject to the whim of fortune; is lucky or unlucky, helped by an invisible hand, or not.

In summary, Defoe's essay defines a project as something that combines public good and private advantage; is of such high risk that it is most likely to come to nothing; and is dependent upon fortune or providence for success that cannot be controlled or planned for. The only criterion of success is success itself, a tautology that grounds the act of projecting on nothing more than projections. The Bank of England, nowadays materialized as timeless rusticated stone, was originally no more than some conversations in a coffeehouse concerning a speculative merchant bank. This was a project to support merchants in their own ventures and the country in its hugely speculative bid to defeat the French. As Nicholson declares, the Bank was the foremost project of the age.[9] *Moll Flanders* was also a commercial and civil project, an act of imagination that became material. 'Writing', Defoe explains, 'is become a very considerable Branch of the English Commerce. The Booksellers are the Master Manufacturers or Employers. The several writers, Authors, Copyers, Subwriters, and all other Operators with pen and ink are the workmen employed by the said Manufacturers'.[10] Langelot de Fresnay, writing in 1713, describes 'a sort of Frenzy in writing and Reading' of secret histories and novels. The English translator added the note: 'This is nowhere so notorious as in England'.[11] *Moll Flanders* and the Bank of England are early successes of this frenzy of projects and projecting, their early instabilities and indiscretions now forgotten. Success has sanctified them.

There is tremendous ambivalence expressed in the *Essay*

towards projects, projecting and projectors. Its complexity mocks present-day accounts of the entrepreneur as a brave hero whose abilities will save the nation. Defoe offers a short history of projecting which compares it to pimping. He declares that the 'planting of foreign colonies' led to the forming of

> joint-stocks, which, together with the India, African, and Hudson Bay Companies, before established, begot a new trade which we call by a new name stock-jobbing... This upstart of a trade, having tasted the sweetness of success which generally attends a novel proposal, introduces the illegitimate wandering object I speak of, as a proper engine to find work for the brokers. Thus stock-jobbing nursed projecting, and projecting, in return, has very diligently pimped for its foster-parent, till both are arrived to be public grievances, and indeed are almost grown scandalous.[12]

Projectors are presented as creative tradesmen and simultane-ously as 'contemptible' tricksters: both heroes and villains. From the early seventeenth century onwards, the projector had been a very suspicious character – 'the rentseeker who pretended public service to pursue their self-interest ... a deluded dreamer advancing wild and impossible schemes, or a relentless conman defrauding others through bogus schemes'.[13] Often associated with illegitimate monopolies granted by a credulous crown, and with a refusal to reveal secret inventions without substantial payments, Defoe's essay needs to be read in this context. It is an attempt to (at least in part) rehabilitate a character who was generally regarded to be a mountebank. So Defoe tells us that projectors can themselves be honest or can employ *deceptio visus* and *legerdemain*, sleights of hand that can be seen as tricks of the trade and hence required skills for any projector. So, for example, Defoe admits: 'All foreign negotiation, though to some it is a plain road by the help of custom, yet it is in its beginning all project, contrivance, and invention'.[14] Projecting is presented as an 'art' but sometimes a dark art dealing in dangerous desires. The Tower of Babel, after all, challenged the authority of God who rewarded such hubris by scattering its projectors over the face of the earth. The builder of the bell tower in Melville's short story which we used as our epigraph is eventually crushed by his bell. Defoe suggests that these ambivalences are integral to projecting, and our story demonstrates too that dark arts are a requirement of any successful project.

Our account of how *Moll* and the Bank emerged suggests further criteria by which to understand the nature of a project. Primary amongst these is the understanding that a project is itself a process of emergence, a pre-history before something is realized; something that comes before. The word 'project' comes from the Latin *projectum* from the verb *proicere* – 'to throw something forwards' – which in turn comes from the prefix *pro-*, denoting something that precedes the action of the next part of the word in time, and *iacere*, meaning 'to throw'. Etymologically, the word 'project' thus originally meant 'something that comes before anything else happens'. In the alchemical tradition, the 'powder of projection' was a version of the philosophers' stone, a catalyst that could help turn base metals into silver and gold. In this book, we are ourselves projecting, throwing forth. We are exploring unknown territory, taking a chance on a hunch and hoping that providence, or you, gentle reader, will favor the blind and the brave. The project, will in the end, be measured by its success, this project on projects. If our dark arts are successful, and our hands stay hidden, you will be changed, and mere words will become gold.

The novel

Comparing the novel to a corporation may seem a bizarre idea, because we would normally assume that they belong to different categories, but a brief reflection brings out many obvious similarities. First, in terms of our everyday experience, being in an organization is rather like being in a novel. There are characters who can be seen as heroes or villains; there is a main plot, which may or may not be the plot first intended, with numerous subplots threatening to dislodge it; there are metaphors and images which shape perception and meaning; there is dialogue which moves the plot along or expresses character; there are narrative viewpoints which take or give power and control over the account; there are crises, adventures, risks and subterfuge. Finally, and just like the publishing of a novel, there is capital investment, distribution and a market to measure profit and loss. These are all important enough as similarities, but we want to show that there are also more profound connections here which are related to how a novel and an organization 'work'. This has to do with the mechanisms that allow them to gain credibility through the techniques that they employ, the expectations that they generate, and the needs they create and fulfil. From this perspective the novel and the organization seem to operate in similar ways, which is the comparison that drives this book.

The literature on the early novel is fundamentally developmental in its search for origins and stages. It centers on the idea of a beginning or significant moment of transformation in the development of the modern novel, which is deemed, though not without contention, to have occurred in the early eighteenth century. Our argument takes its lead from this literature and is thus historical in its beginnings. We assume that there is a moment of alchemy or transformation in the history of the novel around the turn of the seventeenth century, and that this is related to the frenzy of projection that also happens at that time. It seems to us that the time of the beginnings of corporations, adventures and monopolies is related to the beginnings of the idea of the novel, of new ways of thinking about how fictions might become facts. Further, we think that an understanding of the processes involved has the potential to question the taken-for-granted assumptions that underpin both of these institutions at the present time. By exploring how they emerged, how they came into being, we identify fundamental or primary requirements of how they operate, and show that these are actually very similar indeed. To put it very simply, corporations are fictions, and novels create worlds.

It might be thought that our initial position here assumes that 'the novel' can be approached as a coherent form or genre. This is by no means certain. The godfather of cultural studies, Raymond Williams, claims that 'the novel is not so much a literary form as a whole literature in itself'.[15] Attempts at defining the novel have been fraught with controversy because – tautologically – they largely depend on how we define 'the novel' in the first place. To define a novel, you first have to decide what a novel is. The OED settles for 'A long fictional prose narrative, usually filling one or more volumes and typically representing character and action with some degree of realism and complexity'. Some form of realism is a cornerstone of the novel *if* the novel is viewed as beginning in the early eighteenth century. If the novel is defined only as a prose fiction of some length then a case can be made, as Margaret Doody demonstrates, to locate the first novels in Greece[16]. If one defines the novel as essentially a romance, a romantic adventure which ends happily, then one can locate its origins in the 'roman' of France. For our purposes, we will concur with the OED, and accept that the form of the novel involves some commitment to 'realism'. Not that this is a simple view of representing a real world with blunt empirical instruments and direct language. As Williams comments, 'The old naive realism is in any case dead, for it depended on a theory of natural seeing which is now impossible. When we thought we had only to open our eyes to see a common world, we could suppose that realism was a simple recording process'[17]. Realism, in other words, is a genre too. It is a way of seeing and of representing, not an avoidance of artifice. Realism as a cornerstone of the novel was initially proposed by Ian Watt in his iconic text *The Rise of the Novel*. While accepting that Watt might have oversimplified the realism of the novel, we think that his characterization still has enormous value.

Watt begins by suggesting that the novel was new in that it did not rely on historical plots or characters, as Shakespeare or Milton had done, but created its own characters and plots which were then judged as 'valid' or 'true' by how realistic they were considered to be. This form of realism is achieved by detailed descriptions that place people in a particular spatial and temporal setting, and characters are given credible, contemporary names, as opposed to names that echo legend or history. Finally, the style of writing and the language used is a version of everyday speech and commentary, as opposed to the stylized structures of poetry, drama, opera and so on. Realism, in other words, is achieved through a series of innovations that produce a particular effect, and this allows Watt to present the novel as making a distinct and radical break with the past. Michael McKeon, in his *Origins of the English Novel*, accepts key points of Watt's argument but balances discontinuities with continuities and so undermines the triumphalism of Watt's vision of the novel as the defining genre of the modern age. McKeon's more dialectical approach suggests that genre has to be seen as part of history because all new genres and styles must grow from established ones. He takes each of Watt's key points and shows how the shift or change described is dependent for its meaning on a past form and so exists only in a dialectical relationship with an older set of ideas. So, for McKeon, the novel can be seen as a reaction to the old romances. It grew out of the traditional lives of the Saints, the accounts of Christian pilgrimage and of scientific discovery, travel writing, letter writing and so on. All this fed into the possibilities of the novel, but the old also feeds off the new, reinventing and replenishing itself, so we could just as well say that the novel can be seen as a romance which has revamped its style to deal with a more empirical age.

The debate over the exact nature of the transformation of prose fiction in the early eighteenth century nevertheless confirms a general consensus: that the English novel emerged at this time. There are several respected texts that, having reviewed the literature available, proceed with a concept of the novel as a genre developing in the early eighteenth century.[18] Of course, the acceptance of this assumption carries a lot of epistemological baggage, which is summarized by Deirdre Lynch and William B. Warner:

> Introducing the eighteenth century "origins" of "the novel", we validate the assumption that what novels are now was already immanent in what they were then. We ratify geopolitical boundaries (between, for example, England and France). We legislate for a canon of exemplary, "truly" novelistic texts and legislate against popular practices of reading and writing. These are problems endemic to efforts to ascribe a distinct, essential nature to the novel.[19]

The idea of a genre is a limiting device, in other words. It is a way of classifying a particular practice or institution that makes all sorts of assumptions about the evidence for and limits of that practice, as well as tending to assume that we can understand the past through the lens of the present. In summary, whether the English novel 'began' in the eighteenth century is arguable but pretty much everyone would agree that it was a transformational moment in its development.

Literary and historical work on the development of the English novel often begins with *Robinson Crusoe*, which Defoe published in 1719, twenty-two years after the *Essay upon Projects*. It is generally understood as representing and reflecting the development of economic individualism as a major concern of the novel as a genre. Remember that Robinson Crusoe was not entirely fictional. In 1704, a Scotsman called Alexander Selkirk had been marooned for over four years on Màs-a-Tierra, in the Juan Fernandez Islands off the coast of Chile. He was rescued by a privateer, Captain Woodes Rogers, in 1709, later the author of *A Cruising Voyage Round the World* (1712), which Defoe read.[20] In 1724 Captain Charles Johnson (sometimes also supposed to be Daniel Defoe) published the first volume of his *General History of the Robberies and Murders of the Most Notorious Pyrates, and Also Their Policies, Discipline and Government*. The author of the *General History*, published five years after *Robinson Crusoe*, could easily have been Defoe, or could have been the Charles Johnson who wrote the play *The Successful Pyrate*, first performed in 1712. No one seems to know. It could also have been the author of other accounts of piracy now commonly attributed to Defoe, since his name was almost never attached to his work during his lifetime, such as *The King of the Pirates* (also 1719), *The Life, Adventures and Piracies of Captain Singleton* (1720), *Colonel Jack* (1722), *A New Voyage Round the World* (1724) and *The Four Years Voyages of Captain George Roberts* (1726). As with any projectors, the mystery seems appropriate, and entirely consonant with others who have written of strange lands, outlaw bands in forests and even utopias.

As is common in the accounts of projectors, the fiction becomes the fact. Màs-a-Tierra was renamed 'Isla Robinson Crusoe', and 'Captain Johnson' became the inspiration for a thousand books and films. While recognizing the importance of *Robinson Crusoe*, and its many similarities with our theme, we have chosen to study *Moll Flanders*, Defoe's second novel, because its subject matter meshes more closely with the backdrop of this book: the growth of London and money. We are not alone in our preference. Virginia Woolf described *Moll* as one of 'the few great English novels which we can call indisputably great'.[21] The introduction to the Oxford Classics version of *Robinson Crusoe* (1972) concedes that '*Moll Flanders* has gained in popular and critical prestige and has come to replace *Robinson Crusoe* as the most representative, if not the best, of Defoe's fiction and that appealing most to modern taste'.[22] Ian Watt declares that *Moll Flanders* 'imposes itself as the best single work for the purpose of investigating Defoe's methods as a novelist and his place in the tradition of the novel'.[23]

Moll Flanders was written to be a best-seller and it is a rollicking good read, full of adventure: sexual, criminal and financial. There are whores, thieves, pimps, highwaymen, convicts, priests and more crowded into its pages, over which the hulk of Newgate Prison presides with a dark threat. 'Newgate; that horrid Place! My very blood chills at the mention of its Name', cries Moll.[24] Moll herself is an unforgettable character, a true survivor who, no matter what the world throws at her, comes back scheming her way out of trouble with imagination and daring. Born in Newgate itself, her early story is unknown even to Moll, but having been looked after for some time by gypsies, she is separated from them and is lucky enough to be taken on by the parish of Colchester. She determines that she will not follow the usual path from such a poor beginning into servitude but will become 'a gentlewoman'[25] and this she ultimately achieves, albeit through sexual liaisons, illicit marriages both bigamous and incestuous, and finally straightforward theft. She is caught and returned to Newgate where she apparently experiences true repentance. Having escaped hanging she is transported to Virginia where she consolidates her wealth and her relationship with her lover, Jemy.

The mature and successful Moll, we are asked to believe, wrote down her memorandums as a warning to others, and the purveyor of the tale has made these memorandums fit to be read by respectable people like ourselves, like you, gentle reader. As Defoe says in the preface: 'None can without being guilty of manifest Injustice, cast any Reproach upon it, or upon our Design in publishing it'. G.A. Starr, editor of the most recent Oxford Classics version, observes that the number of 'reprints, piracies, and "continuations" by other hands indicate that *Moll Flanders* was an immediate success'.[26] Its success continues because, by any measure, Defoe's novel has been a project smiled upon by fortune, giving rise to multiple editions, films, a musical, TV shows and a voluminous critical commentary. The projection that was *Moll* has prospered, just as the idea of the novel itself has prospered in the intervening three centuries.

The corporation

The same can be said of the Bank of England, a venture incorporated in 1694 and therefore of the same time period as *Moll*. Daniel Defoe (1660–1731) and William Paterson (1658–1719), the founder of the Bank, were friends and co-projectors, entangling their biographies and their creations. Paterson, a Scot, proposed to establish a Bank to provide funds for King William III (William II of Scotland) to fight the French and protect trade routes. His project was both straightforward and radical. £1,200,000 (more than £100 million in today's values) was to be raised by subscription and paid to the King via the Treasury. The money was to be lent at 8 per cent interest and the subscribers would be incorporated in order to manage 'the perpetual Fund of interest' therefore produced. In this way the 'National Debt' was born, an act of imagination that continues to exist in the present day and which has grown to be the major instrument for state policy. In 1694 it was agreed that the government would pay a further £4,000 per year for the management of the fund and would allow the Bank certain privileges. The interest would be paid out of levies on ships' tonnage and wine and beer. It proved an enormous success. The historian John Giuseppi reports that the books for subscriptions were 'opened at "Mercer's Chappell" in the Poultry in London on 21 June; more than £300,000 was subscribed on the first day and the whole sum was completed by 2 July'.[27]

The Bank was a foremost project of this projecting age. The

Bank was one of the early commercial shareholder organizations. There is evidence that the Swedish 'Stora Kopparberg' (Great Copper Mountain) company had issued shares in 1288, but the first charted joint stock company is usual seen as the English 'Muscovy Company' in 1555. (It was originally founded four years earlier, as the deliciously named 'Mystery and Company of Merchant Adventurers for the Discovery of Regions, Dominions, Islands and Places Unknown'.) The Dutch and English East India companies are well known examples from the seventeenth century, but the Bank is one of the early British corporations to offer limited liability. Historians such as John Brewer and P.G.M. Dickson have illuminated the financial revolution which took place at this time, and 'have located the Bank at the very heart of the various economic and fiscal processes that contributed to the emergence of Great Britain as a first-rank imperial and military power, supported by unrivalled and sophisticated systems of state bureaucracy and public finance'.[28] Adam Smith in his 1776 treatise on *The Wealth of Nations* reflects that the Bank acted 'not only as an ordinary bank, but as a great engine of state'.[29] This is an image it retains, as its website currently proclaims:

> The Bank of England is the central bank of the United Kingdom. Sometimes known as the "Old Lady" of Threadneedle Street, the Bank was founded in 1694 with a founding charter that stated its purpose was to "promote the public good and benefit of our people.[30]

In practice the Bank sets interest rates in order to attempt to manage inflation and controls part of the money supply – coins, paper and virtual. Since 1997, it also now has renewed responsibility for maintaining financial stability, though the effect of commercial banks generating money as debt means that the Bank of England has limited control, as the crash of 2008 clearly indicated.

Inherent in our argument is an assumption that the corporation can be approached as a genre of organizing in a similar vein to the novel. This requires some justification and exploration, but is complicated by the fact that origins have not been of the same concern to organization theorists as literary theorists. It is difficult to say when the first organization was founded because it depends entirely on what we mean by 'organization'. Would it, for example, include the arrangements that built the Pyramid of Cheops, around 4500 years ago? Or whatever form of finance, labor supply, technical expertise and coordination built a gothic cathedral? There have been attempts to define what an organization is, but all suffer from the general problem that the word can nowadays generally refer to everything which isn't a state – including armies, churches, small businesses, partnerships, cooperatives and, of course, corporations. Take, for example, the argument put forward by the economist Ronald Coase in his much cited paper 'The Nature of the Firm'. Coase sets out with the premise that 'Economic theory has suffered in the past from a failure to state clearly its assumptions'. His task in the article therefore is to search for the 'definition of a firm' and to explore why firms exist at all. If the economic system works itself, he asks, why does it require coordination?

> As D.H. Robertson points out, we find "islands of conscious power in this ocean of unconscious co-operation like lumps of butter coagulating in a pail of buttermilk." But in view of the fact that it is usually argued that co-ordination will be done by the price mechanism, why is such organization necessary? Why are there these "islands of conscious power"?[31]

Coase concludes that there are costs involved in the price mechanism. If these costs can be reduced by setting up a firm, then, he argues, a firm will emerge. His account of the firm is strictly confined to an economic explanation for the emergence of the business organization as something that congeals as a result of market pressures, but it could be generalized to other forms of organization too. The metaphor of an organization as a lump of butter coagulating in a pail of buttermilk is as compelling as any definition then or since.

In general, organization theory tends to assume 'organization' as a precondition, rather than studying how an organization comes to be. As Jerome Katz and William B. Gartner observe in a paper discussing the properties of emerging organizations, 'our theories and definitions about organizations assume that they already exist; that is, the starting point for our theories begins at the place where the emerging organization ends.'[32] Organization is a most multiplicitous word, one that can be applied to entities as different as the University of Leicester, Walmart and the Mafia, as well as whatever built the pyramids. And this is only the beginning. It can also refer to a system of organizing, such as the economic or military organization of any particular state or territory; a process of organizing, as when describing the organization of an event; or even the organization of an organization. Commentators switch between these meanings at will and without warning. As Alison Pullen and Carl Rhodes comment, 'What is called organization studies defies formal definition because of the breadth and incommensurability of activity that goes on under its name'.[33]

Organization could be understood as an umbrella term that subsumes other options such as the firm, company, enterprise, institution or corporation. Each of these terms carries its own nuances. The British Royal family is known as the 'firm', but the etymology comes to us from making something solid through a signature, as in 'affirming'. The word 'company' suggests a gathering of people, an image played on in the title of Paul Seabright's 2010 book *The Company of Strangers: A Natural History of Economic Life*. 'Enterprise' comes from the idea of taking something in hand, rather like the now-antiquated way of referring to organizations as 'undertakings'. 'Institution' suggests the founding of something permanent; etymologically it means the founding of something that stands, and hence an arrangement that will last. Finally, 'corporation' invokes the body through the legal act of incorporation, the making of one thing from many. Organization, as a generic concept, embraces all of these terms for associating and solidifying human bodies and their actions, as well as various materials, but lurking in this multiplicity nowadays there is a core metaphor at work, that of an arrangement with some sort of formal rules. This necessarily conjures images of the bureaucracy, of a body of people and machines being coordinated from the desks of managers. This, we think, is the default image of the organization in the present age, despite the best efforts of theorists who have tried to claim that contemporary organizations are networked, post-bureaucratic and virtual.

Such assumptions are nicely brought out by the economist Mark Casson in his discussion of the theory of the firm. He concludes by asking:

> What is an organization? An organization, in our sense, is any stable pattern of transactions between individuals or aggregates of individuals. Our framework can thus be applied to the analysis of relationships between individuals or between subunits within a corporation, or to transactions between firms in an economy. Why do organizations exist? In our sense, all patterned transactions are organized. When we ask "why do organizations exist", we usually mean to ask "why do bureaucratic organizations exist" and the answer is clear. Bureaucratic organizations exist because, under certain specifiable conditions, they are the most efficient means for an equitable mediation of transactions between parties.[34]

The contemporary image of the organization has at its core this image of the bureaucracy, a large-scale hierarchically organized entity that has lots of employees and lots of rules, and probably occupies some large buildings. All our contemporary ideas about organizations are measured against this for variation, although this assumption is rarely stated. For example, popular ideas about organizations being 'flexible' assume the backdrop of an ideal typical bureaucracy and not the construction industry, the circus or organized crime, each of which has always needed considerable flexibility in employment practices and the spaces and times of their operation.

It is often suggested that contemporary organization theory is engaged in a long debate with the ghost of Max Weber, who pretty much defined our conceptions of what it means to be ruled by people who sit at desks and keep files, rather than people who carry swords or scepters. In his posthumously published 1922 book *Economy and Society*, as well as other work, Weber outlines different forms of legitimate authority, one of which is based on rational grounds 'resting on a belief in the "legality" of patterns of normative rules and the right of those elevated to authority under such rules to issue commands'.[35]

Weber suggests that the legal-rational authority underlying a bureaucratic administrative structure is characterized by general obedience to a consistent system of abstract rules, as opposed to legitimacy being based on the charisma of particular individuals, or unchanging traditions which are passed down through the generations. This is rule from the desk, or more precisely, from the rule-book. The person in authority occupies an 'office', which means that they are themselves also subject to an impersonal order to which their actions are oriented. Importantly though, any person has authority only as a member of the organization. This means that, for all members of a bureaucracy, obedience and duty are to the impersonal order rather than the person. Weber saw the character of bureaucracy as world-changing in its capacity to produce a new form of social order, but also as something which might crush the human spirit, producing people who act like cogs in machines, and are stripped of passion and care.

The widespread application of Weber's thought in the first two thirds of the twentieth century suggested that the development of modern forms of organization was nothing less than identical with the development and continual spread of bureaucratic administration and a Fordist economy. Early management theorists such as Taylor, Gantt and Fayol, as well as state technocrats and consultants of various kinds, described the growth and organization of commerce, corporations, the state, political parties and so on in terms of the spread of legal rational ideas. Organizations, it was suggested, were rational and ordered, and produced a rational and ordered world. Even the 'alternatives' explored since the 1960s – post-bureaucracy, post-industrialism, the virtual organization, post-Fordism, the information society and so on – measure themselves against bureaucracy. It seems to us that what unites all the forms of organization generally accounted for in organization theory is some sense of a bureaucratic administration to which they conform, aspire or stand against. 'Organization' nowadays carries the metaphor of the solidified bureaucracy, and hence limits the imagination in regard to the complexities and possibilities of organizing. Perhaps more importantly, though, it also privileges the rational as a foundational metaphor, and rationality as the prime mover. That is to say that acts of organizing – of making rules for the arrangement of humans and things in time and space – are registered as the primary and only real function of the entity, the organization.

In contrast, we think that our account of Defoe, Moll and Paterson allows us to tell a different story, one that begins not with rationalization, but with projectors, and all the moral and financial risks associated with imagination. Organizing, as a verb as well as a noun, suggests that both the novel and the organization are dynamic fictional processes that begin with hazard and deceit. Our story hence begins with the organic, rather than the mechanical, with romantic fictions and not the machineries of reason. It also allows us to emphasize a series of tensions between order and disorder, or entity and process, which are played out in this book. The suffix '-ization' usually indicates that a process is at work that counters the root word. So feminization suggests that something is being made feminine which is not initially feminine. We would like to suggest that rationalization means something is being presented as rational, or made rational, which is not rational in its origins. In these terms, organization suggests an activity that is pretending to be something that it is not, that is becoming organized from some originary state of chaos. It is a noun that contains its shadow, and tries to suppress disorganization. To what does it pretend? (To employ the eighteenth-century meaning of that word.) It pretends to the instrumental, the rational and the structured, to order, and it pretends an ability to produce that order.

As we said, there is very little literature available on the history of 'organization' as such. There is certainly no search for origins on the scale of Watt or McKeon's work on the beginnings of the novel. The few texts that do exist focus specifically on the history of the commercial company, or the corporation. The business historians John Micklethwait and Adrian Wooldridge in *The Company, a short history of a revolutionary idea*, locate the origins of the company in the mid-nineteenth century. As with the novel, the moment of origin depends on the definition. They declare that there are two ways in which this might be done:

> The first is merely as an organization engaged in business: this definition as we shall see, includes everything from informal Assyrian trading arrangements to modern leveraged buy-outs. The second is more specific: the limited-liability joint-stock company is a distinct legal entity, endowed by government with certain collective rights and responsibilities.[36]

So joint stock companies are clearly not the beginning of commercial organization because we can find formal businesses ás far back as 3000 BC in Mesopotamia. The Phoenicians and later the Athenians spread similar organizations around the Mediterranean. Indeed, the Romans can also stake a claim:

> William Blackstone, the great eighteenth-century jurist, claimed that the honor of inventing companies "belongs entirely to the Romans." They certainly created some of the fundamental concepts of corporate law, particularly the idea that an association of people could have a collective identity that was separate from its human components. They linked companies to the familia, the basic unit of society... The Firms also had some form of limited liability.[37]

If we take Micklethwait and Wooldridge's second definition then companies begin with the medieval merchant empires of Italy and the state-chartered corporations and guilds of northern Europe. Anthony Sampson proposes that the forerunners of today's corporations

> were the merchant companies which grew up in the north west of Europe in the seventeenth century, supported by governments which granted them monopolies in return for taxes. The long voyages of the Muscovy Company to Russia, or the Levant Company to the Middle East, were too expensive for any single investor to finance, so they joined together in 'joint-stock companies' which became increasingly effective.[38]

But Micklethwait and Wooldridge identify the Victorian era as the true origin of the companies that they are interested in. The figures support their contention. In the period between 1856 and 1862 five thousand limited liability companies were incorporated in the UK. These emerging companies combined the original idea of a joint-stock company forged in the seventeenth century with the new unrestricted idea of limited liability to protect the interests of shareholders. Micklethwait and Wooldridge locate the revolution of their book's title here, citing Peter Drucker's study of the corporation in support:

> This new 'corporation', this new Societe Anonyme, this new Aktiengesellschaft, could not be explained away as a reform, which is how the new army, the new university, the new hospital presented themselves. It clearly was an innovation ... It was the first autonomous institution in hundreds of years, the first to create a power centre that was within society yet independent of the central government of the national state.[39]

It is clear that the origin of *the* organization, whether commercial or not, can no more be sought out than can the origin of the novel; organizing and storytelling have always been with us. However, we wish to place a more significant emphasis on the seventeenth century than Micklethwait and Wooldridge. We will argue that there was a moment of transformation in the nature of the modern English organization around the end of the seventeenth century which happened at the same time as a key moment of transformation in the development of the English novel. The Bank of England creates and reflects this transformation as it establishes itself as an organization that exists over and above personal and traditional authority. Its validity and credibility is established by being seen as separate from the traditional authorities of the church or monarch. It is to a large extent founded upon its own projections. These are the revolutionary principles elaborated by Micklethwait and Wooldridge and they are present in the formation of the Bank of England. The Bank established a level of independence as a Company, independent of King, clerics and Parliament, which was unprecedented. This, it seems to us, was a new form of social arrangement that established characteristics that would later be inherited by the companies established in the Victorian era.

To some degree Micklethwait and Wooldridge accept this premise. That being said we must also acknowledge that the idea of the joint-stock company suffered a hiatus because of the particular disasters of the South Sea Bubble and the fall of the Mississippi Company, which brought the model into even more disrepute and ushered in the 'Bubble Act' of 1720. This prohibited the joint-stock form of company unless it was specifically authorized by royal charter. This law was not repealed until 1825, allowing the rapid explosion of joint-stock companies in Victorian times. Yet, despite this century of state intervention against the problems of the projector, it can safely be argued that the seventeenth and early eighteenth century was a key moment in the formation of the modern English organization, and the Bank of England was a foremost example of this new model. We think that the idea that imagination could become independent of its creators, that a projection could become embodied, incorporated, gains a particular intensity in this era.

This book

This little book could belong to quite a few different disciplines. History, management, literature; or more specifically, cultural history, organization studies, literary theory and so on. This presents us with some problems, because whatever we do, we will fall into gaps, or be deemed insufficiently embedded within this or that set of literatures or debates. This book can never satisfy the requirements of all these fields, all these interminable rules of evidence and citation that allow us to understand what counts as knowledge within a particular discipline. This situation poses a number of questions for this book. Who will validate it? Who will read it? What register does it require?

We could take the highly complex style of much literary criticism in which critics, and this is the operative word, politely 'damn with faint praise' their predecessors, and tend to celebrate their own sophistication. Or, we could write with the adolescent fervor of many management and organization theorists who trash all who have gone before as false deities or fools, only to set themselves up as the new well-compensated experts. Neither appeals. In fact a register in and of itself is problematic, suggesting a limiting device which is required to facilitate acceptance by a closed circuit of readers or followers. In academic life, this has become increasingly the situation. Thousands of pages of print and pixel are produced on a daily basis by academics to be read and judged by other academics, or published in books that only libraries can afford to buy. We want to do something different here, and to write in a way that allows a wide range of people to be able to read this book easily, and find something useful in it. This demands a register that is accessible, and doesn't embed itself in disciplinary controversies or technical terminology. Like Defoe, who earned his living on Grub Street, we want to be read.

In *The Romantic Economist*, Richard Bronk attempts the same feat. Bronk tries to find a style suitable to a wide audience, and garners support for this approach in historical attempts to challenge specialist language, quoting the argument of the essayist William Hazlitt, a contemporary of Wordsworth:

> For Hazlitt, the problem was not only that such prose is a barrier to its being read by non-specialists, but also that the very precision and abstraction it represents helps preclude a more comprehensive understanding of the human predicament. This reminds us that the beauty of language in its every day form is that by being less precise and abstract than philosophical or economic language – that is, by being more fluid, suggestive and yet grounded in common experience – it is, paradoxically, less apt to drain away the complex significance of a situation.[40]

Bronk argues that his challenge to the use of specialist language and frameworks is 'crucial to the project of the Romantic Economist ... because it helps ensure that the assumptions and methods used by economists, and the way they frame problems, are open to audit by the broader audience'.[41] Defoe also wrote in 'ordinary' language but dealt in, and created, extreme complexity and ambiguity. He was writing for a broad audience, because he wanted to sell books, but also because he wasn't an academic writing for the approval of others like him. Indeed, as we shall see later, he wasn't very impressed with academics, and their mere scholasticism.

In an important sense, this complexity is forced upon us anyway. The language and style of Defoe and Paterson are very much present in *Moll* and in the Bank of England. The dynamics of power and difference that they catalyzed, rode, or managed to harness in some way are inevitably present in the current manifestations of both. Perhaps their 'projects' remain unfinished, unless we imagine that we, now, are witness to the final form of novel and bank. It seems unlikely though that we are writing now at the end of history, and that means that Defoe and Paterson have their invisible hands on what we write, and that our presence in this project, this book, cannot be ignored either. Defoe and Paterson are 'present' in their creations just as we are present in this text, in this story about some things that happened three hundred years ago, and our reflections on what they might mean for us, now.

This is a book that explores differences and distinctions, both historical differences and disciplinary ones. We believe that this is important because exploring difference dislocates meaning and therefore allows new possibilities to come into the world. Exploring difference brings a new awareness of self too. It fractures some assumptions, and allows stories to be told that conjoin the past and the present, as well as management, literature and history. We think that this is good because it discourages closed or group thinking. Assumptions become recognized as such – as assumptions – when people have to explain their views to others from outside their times and spaces. The 'outsider' who carries difference with them is less likely to be committed to preserving boundaries and the power dynamics that sustain them. This means that the outsider is more likely to be oriented to change, to novelty, to being a projector. As we will show, Defoe and Paterson were dislocated outsiders who were able to challenge the power dynamics of the period, particularly by their use of everyday language. So the attempt at inter-disciplinarity here in this book, including the use of more ordinary language, is in many ways an attempt to recover a way of thinking that is characteristic of the end of the seventeenth century. Defoe and Paterson appear to have operated without much of a sense of discipline, of proper times and places for certain activities, of being constrained by there being particular types of writing or of institutions. Guided by their hidden hands, we want to do the same, and throw doubt on the puny distinctions and boundaries that we have made since their time.

The next chapter examines this space of composition, exploring how *Moll Flanders* and the Bank both reflect and create the projecting age. We suggest that a shift in the nature and operation of the imagination took place during this time that fostered the novel and the Bank. They have primary characteristics in common because they met the same problems and solved them using the same techniques. Chapter 3 engages with the revolutionary nature of this period and the ways in which *Moll* and the Bank reflect and create emancipatory events. We suggest that they play their part in shaping a 'democracy to come' and so share characteristics of form and function. Chapter 4 reveals the accidental in the stories of Moll Flanders and the Old Lady of Threadneedle Street, drawing out a sense of the uncanny in their realization, as if an invisible hand guides events. Chapter 5 explores Defoe and Paterson as projectors and finds that their lives are intertwined in much the same manner as their projects. In the conclusion, we discuss the implications of our argument for the study of the novel and the organization, and for writing and organizing more generally. This history has lessons after all, as all good stories should.

2

The Space of Composition

This chapter places *Moll Flanders* and the Bank of England in the historical moment of their emergence and demonstrates that they both reflect and create a transformative shift in the operation of the imagination. This shift is largely fostered by the changing circumstances of the new space of composition. We argue that this space is opened up by the growth of a wide and diverse market, as well as a shift from valuing the tangible, as in land or buildings, to valuing the intangible, as in credit. It also involves an orientation towards the future, rather than the past, including the use of possible futures with which to understand the potentials of the present. This opens a sense of space and time for the imagination. These shifts lead to a frenzy of projects and projecting, of which the novel and the Bank are primary examples. We think that they use the same techniques to operationalize their project, and so make real their projections. That is to say, they operate in similar ways.

The projecting age

Ian Watt, in his 1957 *The Rise of the Novel*, places the texts he is concerned with (the novels of Defoe, Richardson and Fielding), clearly in their context. This was the early eighteenth century, and Watt attempts to discover what the 'favourable conditions in the literary and social situation were'[42] that promoted the emergence of these early novels. He shows how they arose from and reflected their particular moment in history, a moment of radical transformation that echoes through to our present. Watt's text was itself transformational in its time. As J. Paul Hunter reflects, it 'burst onto the scene' with considerable sociological and historical notice.[43] Watt simply dispensed with debates about the origins of the novel with the unassailable argument that 'the appearance of our first three novelists within a single generation was probably not sheer accident'.[44] His discussion of the novel as a reflection and creation of economic and social structures, linking literature to ideology, was profoundly radical in 1957, as well as being rather awe-inspiring because its topic and tone was a sense of wonder at the rise of the novel. The novel is pictured as a wondrous event, a happening, as in the 'rise' of its title, inaugurating a distinct break with the past, a revolution in literature involving realism, the common man, the supremacy of the individual and a challenge to the literati.

Watt's text has since been superseded by Michael McKeon's *The Origins of the English Novel 1600–1740* in 1987. McKeon tempers Watt's account of awe-inspiring change. While accepting the basic premise that the novel came together from the constellations of a particular time period, McKeon approaches its elements more philosophically. So 'realism' becomes the much more complex 'empiricism', and discontinuities are balanced with continuities. He plots the novel's ancestry on a myriad of fronts and there is no triumphant 'rise'. His analysis is profoundly insightful and has rightly influenced all discussion of the novel since its publication. However, we think it is time to reinstate some of the awe inspired by Watt's text and his subject.

It is a subject of wonder that these early novels came to be. The shift in the nature and parameters of literature that they represent was, and is, enormous. So whether we can track its history or not, whether it happened in other countries or not, whether we see the novel as a new form of literature or not, we need to preserve some sense of just how remarkable this new form was at the time. Something transformational happened in these early texts. As Michael Seidel has asserted:

The literary revolution that Defoe's *Robinson Crusoe* helped instigate is monumental. No matter what talk there is of the forebears of the novel, very little reads like a novel until Defoe develops the form beginning with Crusoe.[45]

Like Watt, we want to be able to imagine the magnitude and depth of the changes that took place around this time. The key causal factors he established, such as the reported increase in a reading public and a burgeoning middle class of merchants and their wives, are explored in chapter 3. In this chapter, we are interested in how the economic, political and cultural developments changed the operation of the imagination. This new space of composition opened up new possibilities, and we think that the Bank of England and *Moll Flanders* both emerge from this space. English cities, particularly London, were places of huge violence and displacement at this time. The effects of the enclosures produce the seething poor, with their rookeries and gallows, as well as the emerging bourgeoisie, with their coffeeshops and fevered imaginations.

Space of composition

The 'space of composition' is a concept established by Timothy Clark in his work on the nature of inspiration and creativity. For us, it provides a framework in which to understand the relation between the operations of the imagination and a time period. He describes his book *Inspiration* as:

a study of theories of 'creativity' in Western Literary Theory since the Enlightenment; or to be more precise, of the understanding of the process of composition as the site of a unique, valuable and rare transformation and even revolution of the psyche; in a word, 'inspiration'.[46]

Clark catalogues the various approaches to the concept of inspiration from Plato's image of the poet as a dangerous person possessed by a form of madness, through classical calls to the muses and the Gods. He proceeds onwards to the Romantics' claim to a privileged imagination which sets free explosions of genius, and on to Derrida's sense of poetic inspiration as almost, when engaged with a sense of the 'other', taking down dictation by heart.[47] Clark suggests that inspiration always involves a crisis of subjectivity, a fragmentation of personhood. The concept necessarily contains a tension between the individual creator and a force outside them to which they seem to succumb. This is a very familiar notion in fiction writing, but we think that similar processes can be understood to take place in other projects too, such as organizations. A projector is never in complete control of the project but is always subject to forces outside them which nevertheless need to be captured and controlled in order to realize a successful venture. Individualism matters in creativity, but it is not the only thing that matters.

George Eliot remarked 'that in all that she considered her best writing, there was a "not herself" which took possession of her, and that she felt her own personality to be merely the instrument through which this spirit, as it were, was acting'.[48] Clark himself cites a study by Paul Eggert which surveys accounts of the process of composition from ten Australian novelists. Eggert observes how some 'reach for pseudo-Romantic phrasings in their interviews because they have all experienced the feeling, however briefly, of not being in control, of going with the flow, of writing almost from dictation'.[49] Even J.K. Rowling talks of her distress when the process of writing the *Harry Potter* series 'required' the death of the character of Dumbledore. It is almost as if a hidden hand were directing these writers' actions, making them puppets of other forces.

Clark seeks to locate inspiration as an event that takes place in a particular social space. He argues that the space of composition shapes the act of creativity in that the writer anticipates the response of the audience and so enters a space of action that is outside them:

A recurrent argument of this book is that a writer's conception of a 'creative' 'inner' power is often an image of an anticipated rhetorical effect ... Inspiration in its Romantic form of a state of super-creativity, is an aspect of 'modernity' in the sense of that condition in which the writer 'no longer knows for whom he writes', a situation contemporary with the demise of patronage, the professionalization of the writer and the emergence of mass audiences.[50]

This move to a large, to some degree unknown, market opens up a wider space in which the imagination can operate, challenging the previous boundaries within which a small, elite group dominated the operation and nature of the space of composition or invention. We think that this general sense of opening up is one of the factors that led to the frenzy of invention and projecting discussed in chapter 1. Novak, in his collection of essays on *The Age of Projects*, suggests that many of these projects were 'airy schemes' and unrealizable, but that didn't mean that they were unimportant. The philosopher Leibniz, for example, conceived of the computer but it would take another two hundred years to realize it. Novak concludes that 'the excitement in projecting was an essential and vitalising part of the age'.[51]

Although the term 'the age of projects' is thought to derive from Defoe, the phrase he actually used in his essay was the 'Projecting Age'. As he tells us, 'Necessity, which is allowed to be the mother of Invention, has so violently agitated the wits of men at this time that it seems not at all improper, by way of distinction, to call it the Projecting Age'.[52] Defoe traces the 'original of this projecting humour that now reigns no farther back than the year 1680'. He locates the origins of projecting in inventiveness, contending that although other ages have experienced some 'humour of invention', none have come to 'the degree of projecting and inventing' seen in the period in which he lived.[53]

Though, as we have seen, the word 'projector' was being used fifty years previously, economic historians support the contention that this was a period of particular innovation. Joel Mokyr, in *The Enlightened Economy*, describes the early eighteenth century as a period of extraordinary and widespread inventiveness in Britain:

> Innovativeness in the decades around 1700 was not confined to factories or the few other large scale enterprises such as shipyards or mines. Even the cottage industries, where production took place in workers' homes, were capable of technological progress ... and many of the inventions we associate with the factory system were first tried in small-scale workshops.[54]

Mokyr is also keen to share his wonder at the inventiveness of this period:

> Economic accounts of this period have tended to describe this transformation as a success story, opening themselves up to charges of "triumphalism." I will make a conscious effort to avoid such pitfalls in this book, but I will probably fail to some extent. The dilemma that a historian asked to describe this process faces is obvious: can one and should one tell this tale without stressing that by most criteria – not least those of people living at the time – this was an astonishing success story?[55]

As we noted in chapter 1, writing projects also proliferated. There was a: 'Frenzy in writing and Reading', a flurry of secret histories, travel stories and novels, and nowhere more so than in England.[56] The parallel between this frenzy and the economic one seems clear enough, and suggests that the space of composition is opened up for and by people like Defoe and Paterson. They are both inventing commercial projects which are dependent on a much wider range and diversity of market participants than would previously have been possible. This changes the process of imagining, a social context that shapes what individuals can conceive. In the way that Clark presents the process of creativity there is a degree to which individuals step outside of themselves as they anticipate the effects of their projections on a projected audience or market. The author enters a kind of liminal space, a space that is in-between; a moment of origin or genesis before the project is realized. Some theorists have claimed this space as the space of literature, but it seems to us that the Bank is also a project of the very same kind. It requires an absence from which to build its presence, a space in which it can be built.

For example, Maurice Blanchot, the French philosopher and literary theorist, describes the *récit* (narrative) as always trying to merge with its reality or event, but insists that it is the 'ceaseless' merging that is actually its reality.[57] Literature never simply 'is', but is always a process of becoming, of never being the same as reality, but always in a relation with it. We think that this is also the 'reality' of the Bank, whether it is apparent or not. Behind its now monumental walls of stone, it ceaselessly attempts to merge with its narrative, to become the story that it is telling. This suggests that the Bank, and any organization, is always a dealer in projections. The actual 'reality' of an organization can never be pinned down because it is never reducible to its buildings, people, technology and so on. We have never seen an organization, and we never will. Any organization is always a temporary constellation of routines, lying beyond what has gone before, and in between what has been and what may be; it is always a becoming.[58] The Bank and *Moll*, and by implication organizations and the novel, remain, to some degree, in this space of projection, of becoming. They can never be complete for they are always in the business of projecting, of telling stories that construct boundaries between inside and outside.

The question of where and how the Bank exists echoes a

seminal work in literary criticism by M.H. Abrams. In *The Mirror and the Lamp*, published in 1953, Abrams explains: 'The title of the book identifies two common and antithetical metaphors of mind, one comparing the mind to a reflector of external objects, the other to a radiant projector which throws light on the object it perceives. The first of these was characteristic of much of the thinking from Plato to the eighteenth century; the second typifies the prevailing Romantic conception of the poetic mind'.[59] As David Lodge comments in regard to these metaphors, 'the super-session of the former by the latter has far reaching consequences for aesthetics, poetics and literary criticism'[60] – and, we would add, organizations. This period in the early eighteenth century, when the shift to the idea of a creative 'radiant projector' was taking place, is the moment when the novel and the organization emerge, illuminated by and reflecting this movement towards projecting and projection.

The projecting humor

The 'projecting humor' associated with the period reveals not only a difference in the scale of the space of inventiveness at this time but a difference in the nature and qualities of the imagination. The 'projecting humor' is a capacity to imagine, a capacity essentially characterized by an ability to create something out of this open space, almost out of nothing, as human beings become dependent not on a Creator, a King or Bishop, but on making themselves. This transformation in the operation of the imagination is also exemplified by a shift in the attitude to land, wealth and property. In this transformation from feudalism to capitalism, value shifts from being attached to something tangible, land, to something intangible, the specters of capital, which depend solely on credit and credibility, on being believed.

Land had been the basis of wealth for centuries. It was a tangible asset that everyone could see, and which from the early modern period could be and was measured and enclosed so that others could not benefit from it. Land could produce firewood, rabbits, rents, crops and cattle. From this perspective, wealth is finite: there are a limited number of exchanges that can be made with and on the surface of the earth. In the projecting age value shifts to intangibles, to a world of projections and credit, and then wealth appears to become infinite as the number of potential exchanges become infinite. The key arbiter of value in this new intangible world of projections is credit, that is, whether a projection can be believed in or not. The historian J.G.A. Pocock documents the rise of credit in this way:

> The volume of investment meant that the shares, tickets, or tallies entitling the possessor to a share of repayment from the public funds became marketable property, whose value rose and fell as public confidence in the state's political, military, and financial transactions waxed and waned. The fundholder and the stockjobber, the bull and the bear, had come upon the stage; and the figure around which they were grouped, the concept which they introduced into the language of English politics, was not Trade but Credit.[61]

So 'credit', etymologically related to 'credo', in the sense of trust and belief, becomes the new ground for the economic. This shift in the nature of the imagination is also posited by the work of a group of literary critics in the early 1990s, most notably Colin Nicholson, Catherine Ingrassia and Sandra Sherman, who explore the interconnectedness between literature and the financial markets.

Nicholson explores the influence of the new financial forces on the satirical writings of Pope, Gay and Swift who positioned themselves against their times, presenting themselves as part of a group of respected men of letters who stood in a lineage inherited from classical writers. They, sometimes meeting at the 'Scriblerus Club', were alarmed by the new financial forces that threatened to shift the order of social relations, transferring power from land and landowners to new *arriviste* social groups. As Nicholson notes:

> The seemingly perverse and unpredictable relationship between opinion and fantasy and business confidence began to assume the dimensions of a social power, and for the traditionalists such a leap from the politics of domestic economy and landed integrity to the administrative apparatus of modern finance was not at all palatable. As the far-reaching consequences of these developments make their way into imaginative recognitions, Opposition writers generate answerable figures of alien and corrupting forces.[62]

The reaction to this new world often combined fear and hostility, as a seemingly solid world appeared to melt away, and stable feudal understandings of the location of value dissolved. Ingrassia focuses on the notion of paper credit at this time, and draws out the imaginative nature of this turn:

> With new financial institutions, the types of negotiable paper available proliferated: lottery tickets, stocks, bills of exchange, and letters of credit were among numerous forms of "credit"-able paper in circulation. The change in the nature of value systems meant that property became increasingly unreal. The new financial instruments of Exchange Alley were largely immaterial forms of property that could be realised only imaginatively ... The investor had to fantasize or create imaginatively a narrative that invested the purchase with some meaning about the individual stock and the future performance of the market.[63]

Ingrassia draws out a relationship between finance and the novel, arguing that 'activities in the new economic system and pursuits in the literary marketplace were constructed as culturally analogous and can be read as historically contingent symbolic practices that changed individual's understanding of their opportunities for "improvement"'. She observes that the buying of stock and the reading of novels 'demanded of author and reader, or producer and consumer, the participation in or the creation of an imaginatively based narrative', and proposes that 'the development of popular fiction and the acceptance of various narrative conventions naturalised the demands that speculative investment made on participants' imaginations'.[64] Both Nicholson and Ingrassia assume that there is a relationship between fiction and fact, between the imagination that launches narratives and that which launches credit. Both require belief.

Sandra Sherman specifically attempts to 'account' for Defoe and, in common with other authors and historians, finds him curiously absent. Bringing together his non-fiction and fictional writings, she explores the development of ideas about the difference between truth and fable in the early eighteenth century across the discourses of finance and writing. She argues that 'a credit-based market dissipated the author. "Nobody" could be identified with discursive production.' Indeed, she suggests that authors were themselves complicit in this de-authorization, 'foregoing identity to stay in the market, producing fiction for which they could not be held to account'.[65] There are many controversies about authorship and ownership at this time, partly because of the problems with establishing and maintaining copyright, and the attribution of many of Defoe's works is even now still unclear. Authors' names simply didn't appear on the title pages of novels, or in the serials and magazines that often preceded the complete text. As a consequence, Sherman posits that the disappearing author of the discourses of finance and fiction traded in uncertainties which were then employed to maintain the author's anonymity. In many ways, the person who composed, the author of a text, had themselves become a space which allowed for composition. As we will see, this means that the origins of both novel and Bank were effaced, partly to produce effects that looked like truth, but also because there were dangers in being too clearly identified as an author who could be made responsible for their creations, and hence be accused of trading in lies.

Drawing on the work of these writers, it seems to us that there was a shift from working within a space of composition that privileged the authority of God and King arranged across a tangible territory, to an opening up of uncertainty as people searched for new narratives. This new space was both liberating and frightening, making possible and necessary projections of all kinds to fill it. Such a situation invoked huge anxiety, a frenzy of speculations. The Bank of England and *Moll Flanders* are particular examples of this speculative frenzy; examples that successfully solidified and became models for the further development of both the corporation and the novel. They deal in projections and are themselves projections. The Bank of England deals in promises of the future that are essentially made-up, albeit from the probabilities derived from a present reality. *Moll Flanders* is obviously made-up too, albeit from the probabilities derived from a realistic possible situation. An organization is an imaginative projection in pretty much the same way that a novel is an imaginative projection. The next section details the deceits, techniques and practices involved in 'making up' the projections of *Moll* and the Bank.

Projecting *Moll Flanders*

We think that all projects require a certain fictionality, a necessary deceit. *Moll* and the Bank of England are both 'made-up'; they are fictions that work when we believe in them. They use the same techniques to establish credibility, techniques that necessarily verge on the dishonest and so call into question the degree to which transparency or honesty can be seen as legitimate criteria in judging projects at all. Watt stresses that one of the chief criteria of a novel is just this – it is made-up:

> Defoe and Richardson are the first great writers in our literature who did not take their plots from mythology, history, legend or previous literature. In this they differ from Chaucer, Spencer, Shakespeare and Milton, for instance, whom like the writers of Greece and Rome, habitually used traditional plots; and who did so, in the last analysis, because they accepted the general premise of their times that, since Nature is essentially complete and unchanging, its records, whether scriptural, legendary or historical, constitute a definitive repertoire of human experience.[66]

Watt may be over-stating his argument, but a case nevertheless remains. Projections like this, made-up stories, require trickery and deceit to become operationalized; they have to convince a mass market to give them credit if they are to be realized and function. This is not being economical with the truth, or adding a little fiction to the facts; it is lying in the sense of intentional deceit. Moll Flanders does not exist, she is made-up by someone who knew what they were doing. She is a lie and yet we believe in her, we give her credit.

Defoe has been honored with being 'a great, a truly great liar, perhaps the greatest that ever lived'.[67] Indeed, he himself does not avoid the issue: 'this supplying a Story by Invention ... is a sort of Lying that makes a great Hole in the Heart'.[68] Marthe Robert identifies this deceit as the only true convention for the novel:

> For either a story does not pretend to anything else and reveals even in its texture, the conventions to which it has decided to submit; or it masquerades as reality, in which case it must be naturally aware of betraying its intention to delude.

Since the innocent lies are the most obvious, a novel can only be convincingly truthful when it is utterly deceitful, with all the skill and earnestness required to ensure the success of its deception.[69]

Defoe is a master of deception. He sets this story up as a true history, announcing in the Preface that 'The World is so taken up of late with Novels and Romances, that it will be hard for a private History to be taken for Genuine'.[70] Would all his readers understand the level of his deceit? The story is laid out in its entirety on the title page: This 'true' history will tell –

The

Fortunes

And

Misfortunes

Of the Famous

Moll Flanders, and C.

Who was Born in NEWGATE,

and during a Life of continu'd Variety for

Threescore Years, besides her Childhood,

was Twelve year a Whore, five times a Wife

(whereof once to her own Brother), Twelve Year a Thief,

Eight Year a Transported Felon in Virginia,

at Last grew Rich, liv'd Honest,

And died a Penitent,

Written from her own MEMORANDUMS.

This is both an advertisement and a lie masquerading as truth, a conceit that readers might have enjoyed, or perhaps even been taken in by. Robert Mayer in *History and the Early English Novel* reports that there was indeed confusion amongst early readers about whether *Moll* was indeed 'true history' or 'false'.[71] After all, much about *Moll Flanders* could be said to be true, in the sense of being empirically realistic. The streets of London it refers to are real, Newgate is real, the practices that it recounts are real, and Moll herself could be based on numerous well-known female criminals such as Moll King or Mary Carleton. Yet the whole thing is a lie. How do we come to believe the lie, to believe in something, quite simply, made-up?

The opening lines of the novel proper (as opposed to the various preambles), employ several techniques to hook the reader in and establish credibility for something which is made-up. 'My True Name' she declares 'is so well known in the records, or Registers at Newgate, and in the Old-Baily, and there are some things of such Consequence still depending there, relating to my particular Conduct, that it is not to be expected I should set my Name, or the Account of my Family to this Work'.[72] The recognized and established authorities of Newgate and the Old Bailey, of paper records, are used to give credibility to her existence in a circular referentiality that immediately begins to dislocate the reader. The real and the imaginary are blurred, precisely by claiming that she cannot tell us her real name. This is, after all, a credible claim, because no reasonable person would want their real name to be associated with all the sins and crimes that Moll will recount to us.

There is a bold tease in these opening lines. Moll is to narrate her own story, directly to the reader, who is addressed as 'you'. She is a female protagonist who seems to assume that she is addressing a male reader, such as in the coquettish turn of phrase by which she reveals that 'it is not to be expected I should set my Name, or the Account of my Family to this Work ... it would not be proper'. So we learn she is not actually known as Moll in the records of Newgate and the Old Bailey. Some of her 'worst Comrades', who have gone out of the world 'by the steps and the string', knew her 'by the name of Moll Flanders' she tells us, and that will do for the reader 'till I dare own who I have been, as well as who I am'. We are warned, however, that this is not likely to happen until 'after my Death'. In the final event, that is by the end of the book, we never get to know her 'true name'.

These opening lines display a consummate sleight of hand on Defoe's part. 'My True Name' is established as the mystery of the text while we are warned that we will never know it. This establishes the trick of the novel: a promise that we will 'know' intimately a real character who will narrate the story, while simultaneously warning that the promise will not, cannot, be fulfilled. It cannot be fulfilled because the promise is a fiction. This is the psychological contract that is agreed to in the opening lines of this work, and in the opening lines of every novel – what Paul Davies has called 'the invitation to a fictional world'.[73] The contract is stated in particularly bald terms in the opening lines of *Moll Flanders* – we are privileged in that we are to be told the story but it is made clear that we will never know the secret of her real name. The truth of the lie will never be revealed.

We know her as Moll Flanders. Ian Watt points out the power of naming: 'Proper names have exactly the same function in social life; they are the verbal expression of the particular identity of each individual person. In Literature, however, this function of proper names was first fully established in the novel'.[74] As noted above, prior to the novel, characters in histories or plays or epic poems had tended to be drawn from myth or history. Since their tales were well-known, the art was in the telling of that which was already well-established. Moll Flanders marks a huge shift in that the name can be seen as contemporary, the name of a woman from the time. However, the name also draws on some suggestive connotations. The name 'Moll', a contraction of Mary, seems to have had associations with the idea of a disreputable woman, a prostitute, from the sixteenth century onwards. The OED lists the earliest usage in a 1604 quote from Thomas Middleton: 'None of these common Molls neither, but discontented and unfortunate gentlewomen'. 'Moll Cutpurse', based on the criminal Mary Frith (c. 1584–1659) was a character in a well-known play by Middleton and Dekker, first published in 1611.[75] There are a number of other public figures Moll could have been based on too, and we will return to these later in the book.

As for her surname, Flanders was famous for its cloth, and its weavers, many of whom migrated to England from the fourteenth century onwards. Rebecca Elisabeth Connor in *Women, Accounting and Narrative* points up the irony in a scene from the novel in which Moll has just stolen some cloth. 'Not to be overlooked is the symbolism of the contraband, it is Flemish, or "Flanders" lace – the commodity after which Moll is named'.[76] It is an appropriate name for the protagonist who is a trickster, a rogue and a victim in the harsh commercial world of exchange and barter in 1720. Indeed, we are told that Moll's mother was imprisoned for 'borrowing three Pieces of fine *Holland*, of a certain Draper in *Cheapside*', which was why her baby was born in prison. There are connotations of being an outsider too, perhaps part of a family of migrants who had fled Catholic persecution on the continent. Coming to England to make their fortune they found resentment as they competed for English jobs, as well as persecution under Catholic monarchs until the 'Glorious Revolution' of 1688. All of these connotations play into the naming of Moll. As the next section demonstrates, the nature of the Bank employs the same kind of deceit as the novel and uses exactly the same techniques.

Projecting the Bank

The Bank of England used the same techniques to come into being, to realize the projection. Deceit, trickery, or sleight of hand, was needed on several levels. Firstly, the initial proposal for the Bank depended on it becoming a bank of issue – one that could conjure legal tender from thin air. This necessarily challenged the role of the Treasury and the King, William III. The Committee established to review government finances initially rejected the notion that the Bank would be able to issue legal tender and the proposal was dropped. William Paterson realized that some trickery and deceit would be required to get the project off the ground. When he put forward the proposal again in 1694 he had two new supporters, a Lord of the Treasury, Charles Montague, and an eminent merchant, Michael Godfrey. It appears that these two figures effectively managed the Bill through parliament. The timing was crucial because, despite the prior rejection, the King was now desperate for money to fight the war with Catholic France. Paterson himself admitted that the Government adopted his proposal as a 'lame expedient for £1,000,000'.[77] The King had run out of ideas for raising tax. He had even taxed being a bachelor. Yet at the same time trade was increasing and merchants had money that they wished to keep safe or to invest. The King wanted to get access to this money.

Paterson later confesses that the situation 'produced certain narrow and sinister designs no way becoming so noble and universal a work as this'.[78] The founding of the Bank was hidden in the Bill that approved its incorporation. Paterson had taken out of the second proposal, which Montague put before cabinet, any direct reference to the idea that the Bank would be a bank of issue or indeed any mention of a bank at all. Indeed, 'the very name of a bank or corporation was avoided', he tells us, 'though the nature of both was intended, the proposers thinking it prudent that a design of this nature should have as easy and insensible a beginning as possible, to prevent, or at least gradually to soften and remove, the prejudices and bad impressions commonly conceived in the minds of men against things of this kind before they are understood'.[79] He simply proposed that £1,200,000 be raised by subscription and lent to the Government at 8 per cent; the subscribers would then be incorporated in order to manage 'the perpetual Fund of interest' and the Government would pay a further £4,000 per year for management of the fund and allow the Bank certain privileges. The interest was to be paid out of levies on ship's tonnage and wine and beer. Cabinet debated the matter and with Montague's guidance finally agreed that a Bill be put before parliament. The proposal was then tagged on to the end of an ordinary finance bill and bears the following title:

An Act for granting to their Majesties several Rates and Duties upon Tunnage Of ships and vessels, and upon Beer, Ale and other Liquors: for securing certain Recompenses and Advantages, in the said Act mentioned, to such persons as shall voluntarily advance the Sum of £1,500,000 towards carrying on the War against France.[80]

This is a deceit. The Bank is slipped in under the disguise of taxes on beer and wine. It was put forward at the end of the parliamentary session when many Members of Parliament had already retired to the country and hence would not even see the Bill. Parliament was appeased by the insertion of a clause to say that the Bank could not provide funds for the King without its assent. The deceit worked very nicely indeed. As we noted in the previous chapter, the money actually promised to the King was raised within a few days. It was an unprecedented success.

The Bank had to use sleight of hand many times in its early years. It was potentially exposed to damage with the collapse of the South Sea Company in 1720. Investors panicked and there was a run that could have destroyed the Bank. Playing for time, the Bank made all payments in sixpences and shillings so that it would take a long time to count it out. They organized friends to take out large sums and then take the coins round the corner to another teller to be paid back in, slowly. In this way the Bank managed to stagger through to the holiday of Michaelmas and was able to close for a few days. When it opened again, the danger had subsided.[81]

The idea of the Bank had to be projected, given some kind of reality, before people could believe in it and then invest, give it credit. The primary technique, as with Moll, was the power of naming, of constructing reality with words. 'The Governor and Company of the Bank of England' grandly assumes that the Bank of England already exists in that the governor and company are identified as being from it already. What is being projected is already used as a point of reference. At the moment when it comes into being it seems to assume a past, as if it had always been there. As Giuseppi observes, it was 'either a stroke of genius or of great good luck' that it was called the Bank of England rather than of London:

> For there can be no doubt that the title chosen had a profound and fortunate influence not only upon the development of the Bank itself but on that of all other English banking as well. By every precedent save one, it should have been called after the City its foundation. Amsterdam, Genoa and Hamburg are cases in point – Sweden was the exception ... had it flourished as the Bank of London it is at least probable that the merchants of other trading cities, with Bristol at their head, would soon have sought powers to be similarly incorporated.[82]

By calling it the Bank of *England*, its projectors gave it the authority of the nation at the same time as helping to create that nation. The Bank of England sounded large, reliable, enduring. The naming gave it credibility. Intentional naming of organizations was a new phenomenon, in the same way that giving a character like Moll a contemporary rather than classical name was new. Independent commercial entities had not existed in the same way before and so did not need to be given names because their names were already apparent from their origins. Agencies were governmental or royal or divine, whilst the butcher, baker, and candlestick maker were individuals usually working from their house with their family and would be more likely to be identified by an address than a name. The new joint-stock companies, however, had to have a name put on them, and the grander the better.

Just as Moll refers to the established authorities of the Old Bailey and Newgate to authenticate her own story, so the Bank cloaks itself in the authorities of the time. The Act establishing the Bank is approved by the great seal of the King and Queen of England, 25th April 1694, and they are the initial subscribers. The Corporation also creates its own seal in imitation of this emblem of authority and uses a very specific image, that of Britannia sitting on a pile of money. She is Britain personified as a woman. Giuseppi points out that the use of Britannia in this way was quite recent at the time.

> It is true that on coins of the Emperor Hadrian and Antonius Pius she had appeared, bareheaded, holding a spear, and displaying a naked length of sturdy barbarian leg, but all she denoted was the subjection of one more province of Imperial Rome. After the decline of the Roman Empire there is no known instance of the use of Britannia as a symbol until 1667. In that year, Charles II ordered a medallion to be struck upon which she again appeared – presumably as the result of antiquarian research. This time, however, it was not as a captive barbarian maid, but as the tutelary goddess of a sovereign state. Serene and stately, seated on a rock by the sea, she bears on her shield the combined crosses of St. George and St. Andrew.[83]

Britannia can also be found as a character in Elizabethan drama, but the Royal Mint adopted the figure on coinage during the reign of Charles II and her image was well-known by 1694. The Bank's Britannia deliberately drew on this putatively Roman heritage, the spilling bank of coins added to show success in business. Thus the Bank draws on the authority and power of the past, and establishes itself as a timeless national institution. There was a seal designed with this symbol. It is not known who designed the seal and when, but it was certainly already made when the Act was finally passed. However, it was later found to be too heavy to use and was quietly replaced.

Since that time, Britannia has appeared on every printed Bank of England note. Her appearance has changed over the years and usually reflects the style of that period. In depictions she is usually shown with a shield, helmet, cornucopia and resting decorously on a pile of coins but all of those elements have been dropped at one time or another. Her appearance also differs – long hair, short hair, smiles, frowns, faces left, faces right and so on. The Court Minutes Book does not record why Britannia was chosen, but it seems the Bank could have been influenced by the fact that her image had been adopted by the Royal Mint for the halfpenny and farthing coins then in circulation. The Directors of the Bank had already decided on the forms in which they would give receipts for cash deposited with the Bank and one in particular, the Running Cash Note, was the forerunner of the modern bank note. Perhaps by using Britannia they hoped that the Bank's mere paper, a promissory note for actual coin, would be imagined to be related to the Mint's metallic currency and therefore more likely seen as creditable.

The Bank was to provide a public account of itself at all times by keeping detailed records of every subscription, of every payment, giving time, place, date and amount. These accounts were to be authenticated by appointed Commissioners of the Bank.

The Book of the Subscriptions shows first a sum of £10,000 in the names of the King and Queen, followed by 1,267 individuals … As each vellum sheet was completed it was signed for and sealed by two Commissioners and, at the end of the day's takings, the amount subscribed was similarly authenticated. During the ten days or so in which the Book was open forty six pages in all were completed.[84]

The detailed records, counter-signing, the production of documents on ancient vellum note paper, gave the impression that there was a measurable and manageable logic underpinning the Bank, even from its moment of inception. But the grounds for authentication are necessarily circular because the authorization requires that we first admit an author. The Governor and Company are not a Governor and Company unless the Bank exists and the Bank does not exist unless the Governor and Company exist. The subscriptions are creditable because the Commissioners, created by the emerging Bank, give them credit. In fact, many of these subscriptions were not 'real' in that they were not actual money (if we can credit notes and coins with reality). The historian John Clapham reports that £720,000 of the Bank's capital 'existed in the form of subscriber's bonds which rather sanguinely, were reckoned as cash'.[85] This suggests that well over a half of the initial authentication was simply good credit – a belief that somebody would or could pay up if required. Again, the circularity is clear. The bank gained credit, or accounted itself as of value, by giving credit; that is to say, accounting others as having value. The King and Queen put in £10,000, or are said to, and then took out one hundred times that amount.

Just as with the novel, truth is always referenced by a movement towards something else – Newgate, the Old Bailey, history, the 'true name', the King, Britannia, the nation and so on. This is the invitation to participate in a fiction pretending to be a fact which the investors in the Bank and the readers of the novel must accept for the enterprise to succeed. The readers of a novel know that it is made-up but believe in it to make it real. The investors in the Bank know that it is made-up but believe in it to make it real. They sub-scribe, or under-write, placing their names beneath as foundations for the new project. These are joint enterprises that require 'the suspension of disbelief', the phrase coined by Coleridge less than twenty years later.

The plots of novel and bank involve a promise that can never be fulfilled or an investment that can never be realized. Moll will never tell us her 'true name' so the promise of the opening pages can never be realized. In fact, of course, there is no 'true name'. This lie is a condition of the text. The proposal on which the Bank of England is based refers to a 'perpetual fund of interest'. There is no end envisaged and instead a cycle of lending and borrowing is set in motion that can never end without destroying itself. The capital investment could never be repaid until the organization was no longer in existence. At the time, subscribers were buying the debt and the perpetual interest that it would generate. Two hundred and fifty years later, the original capital investment did have to be repaid when the Bank was nationalized in 1946. Of course by then it proved very difficult to track the original investors. Other much bigger and later debts continued of course, and still do. Without such debt, and its permanent fund of interest, the Bank would cease to exist. In 2014 the then Chancellor of the Exchequer announced that he was paying off some other bonds, including some relating to the South Sea Bubble, as well as the First World War. At the end of that year, the UK National Debt (not including any commercial bank debt) was reckoned at £1,483.3 billion, a very big promise indeed.

As with any bank that lends more than it has, there is a kind of magic taking place which allows the same money to be spent many times over. The Bank is assumed to be creditable, to have value and solidity, so money is given to the Bank to give to the King. The King, or government of the day, pays a return on the money which is then passed to the investors. The debt itself becomes of value because it generates income, which means that The Bank is assumed to be less of a bet and more of an institution. More people wish to invest in it or to bank with it and so money starts to circulate. Organizations that borrow money from the Bank are given credit for having invested in or loaned from the Bank of England, and so promises and propositions become real, in an endless process that can only work as long as it is never completed. If everyone asks for their money back, for the promise to be fulfilled, then the game is over.

Catherine Ingrassia draws out this quality and comparison in relation to speculative investment and the novels of Eliza Haywood (1693–1756).

In her fiction, as Michael McKeon accurately describes, 'love is sheer inconstancy, like commodity exchange an endless circuit in which the movement toward completion and consumption, a perpetual imagining of an end which must never come, becomes an end in itself' ... The 'love' relationship within Haywood's fiction, the perpetual imagining of an end which must never come, mirrors the implicit understanding on which speculative investment depends: the continued deferral of complete repayment until a date which will, of course, never arrive.[86]

Clapham too notes that the Bank created an almost magical circle of money-raising which, ultimately, financed the industrial revolution.[87] Each renewal of its charter helped to extend the Bank's capital base. The original subscription had become £10.7 million by 1742, but loans to Government had risen more rapidly, so that by 1749 the Bank was owed £11.6 million. Money or credit/value was for the first time being disconnected from property or land, severed from something tangible and linked now only to speculation, an imaginative enterprise. Theories of wealth generation also supported speculation, movement, and circulation – like the blood around the body. As Pincus notes, Locke's notion that labor created property made property potentially infinite because of the temporal infinity of labor. Such conceptions help to transform England 'from an agrarian to a manufacturing society, from a society bounded by limited raw materials to a society fuelled by the limitless possibilities of human creation'.[88] Speculation involves projections, financial and imaginative; the future is predicted and a price placed on that future which then operates as something real in the market, something that can be bought and sold. This prospect was unnerving to those with vested interests in land, and derided by key people from the literary establishment such as Pope and Swift.

However unnerving, the prospect of easy money, money made from money, was also attractive. In *Writing and the Rise of Finance*, Colin Nicholson has documented how Pope, Swift and Gay all actually invested in the markets they derided. 'So it becomes an interesting reflection upon subsequent canon-formation and the cultural valorisation it encoded', he notes, 'that some of the most remembered voices from a time of the greatest explosion of financial and commercial activity England has hitherto seen, publicly set themselves determinedly at variance with what was happening, while privately seeking profit from it'.[89] In all this wild speculation, this age of frantic projection,[90] the relationship between reality and fiction was shifting. John Gay could ally himself with cultural conservatives, yet lose a huge amount of money in the South Sea Bubble, and make a good deal of money with the fiction *The Beggar's Opera* in 1728. The value of an investment project lay in how realistic its claims to future wealth were seen to be, in how credible its projections were to possible stakeholders. But this isn't the realism of the world we actually recognize; it's a realism of promises, a wishful calculation of what might be.

The very nature of the project of the Bank replicates this idea of something being made-up, something coming from nothing, to a degree that was almost seen at the time as magical. The project of the Bank depended on the idea of debt having value. This was a profound shift in a nation that jailed debtors in Newgate, or allowed them to find a sordid sanctuary in the 'Liberty of the Mint', a district in south London where Moll also lives for a while. More profoundly than anything else, the project of the Bank established the idea of a national debt that could be parcelled and sold as a commodity, thereby making the entire nation into a commercial venture, held together by a bet on the future. A debt is a negative. It is an absence that propels us forward in order to fill its gap. Something for nothing, a future positive for a present negative. This signals a shift in the nature of the imagination, in the relationship between tangible reality and created realities, in the relationship between signified and signifier. This shift is nicely expressed by Defoe in his 1710 *Essay upon Publick Credit*. Credit, he declares, 'gives Motion, yet it self cannot be said to Exist; it creates Forms, yet has it self no Form; it is neither Quantity or Quality; it has no Whereness, or Whenness, Scottie or Habit. I should say it is the essential Shadow of Something that is not'.[91] The Bank and Moll are making it up as they go along – making something out of nothing, offering promises that can never be fulfilled. They are both 'imaginative productions' which work to the extent that they are credited with some sort of credibility.[92] Of course this shift to an idea of credit, based on nothing substantial, created anxiety and uncertainty, so how was this managed in either case?

Promises and risk

The Bank and *Moll Flanders* are essentially conceits that promise much but are premised on fictions. The subscriber or the reader accepts the fiction, the trick and the deceit, because the illusion is necessary for confidence in an uncertain world. *Moll* offers us the opportunity to partake in very risky adventures from the comfort of our armchair. The dangers of the warrens and rookeries of the city, and the moral hazards involved, are experienced at one remove and with the guardianship of a responsible and able narrator, concerned from the outset with the reader's moral well-being.

Thomas Grant Olsen has explored this aspect of *Moll Flanders*, suggesting that the 'pen' imagined in the Preface of the novel keeps the reader safe while allowing them to experience sin.[93] Defoe presents his role as the author or narrator as that of a 'pen', an instrument for scribing and writing, and an instrument with some power. It claims control: 'The pen employ'd in finishing her Story, and making it what you now see it to be', he confides to the reader, 'has had no little difficulty to put it into a Dress fit to be seen, and to make it speak Language fit to be read'.[94] The 'pen' has taken care of the reader and should be trusted. Both reader and pen are distanced from the story which is figured as unreliable and potentially even dangerous.

Yet there is moral purpose in Defoe telling the tale: 'this Book is recommended to the Reader, as a work from every part of which something may be learned, and some just and religious inference is drawn, by which the Reader will have something of Instruction, if he pleases to make use of it'.[95] The wicked parts are there because they have to be. 'To give the History of a wicked Life repented of, necessarily requires that the wicked Part should be made as wicked, as the real History of it will bear'. Defoe is here flattering (and gently mocking) the reader, establishing that the reader is a good person, like the author:

> this Work is chiefly recommended to those who know how to Read it, and how to make good Uses of it, which the Story all along recommends to them; so it is to be hop'd that such Readers will be much more pleas'd with the Moral, than the Fable; with the Application, than with the Relation, and with the End of the Writer, than with the Life of the Person written of.[96]

This is the flattery of a conman, smiling as they relieve you of your cash, and telling you that they understand. It recommends the work to the reader in almost exactly the same terms as Defoe dedicated his *Essay upon Projects* to his patron Sir Dalby Thomas, a successful projector:

This Preface comes directed to you, not as commissioner, &c., under whom I have the honour to serve his majesty, nor as a friend, though I have great obligations of that sort also, but as the most proper judge of the subjects treated of, and more capable than the greatest part of mankind to distinguish and understand them.

Books are useful only to such whose genius are suitable to the subject of them; and to dedicate a book of projects to a person who had never concerned himself to think that way would be like music to one that has no ear.

And yet your having capacity to judge of these things no way brings you under the despicable title of a projector, any more than knowing the practices and subtleties of wicked men makes a man guilty of their crimes.[97]

As with the novel, Defoe allows Thomas to have his cake and eat it. He can take part in projecting without becoming a bad person. The Preface to *Moll* promises the reader that they can take part in the life of a sinner, and visit places that they would rather not go, but without the risk of being condemned as a sinner themselves. As Moll herself tells us at the end of the novel, 'this Account of my Life, is for ... Instruction, Caution, Warning and Improvement to every Reader'. The fear and anxiety in regard to the projecting of *Moll Flanders*, of perhaps even being seen reading such a vulgar novel, is managed for the reader by the parental figure of the editing 'pen'. The early eighteenth-century reader's fear and anxiety in regard to what McKeon terms 'the disintegration of known categories', or recognized authorities, and the possibility of creating an identity from chaos, from desires and fantasies, is managed by transference. The reader's fears are projected, carried away from the self to 'another'.

The Bank similarly offers to manage the uncertainty and risk of the new world, to take on this risky venture (and its moral questionability) for the investor, offering the guardianship of a responsible and able narrator, the Governor. We are taken into uncertain worlds but promised safety. As wealth or money became mobile, detached from land, it became increasingly difficult to know what to do with it, and one of the options was speculation and projecting. This provoked anxiety and uncertainty but also desire and fantasy, as Ingrassia has pointed out. There was tremendous potential to get rich or lose everything, to change one's position in life for good or for ill, as Moll does on many occasions. The project of the Bank of England was a huge risk, but people rushed to invest, to take a stake in it with cash or promises of cash to come.

Trust was required, but this could only be produced if risk was seen to be minimized. The trust in this case, the paternal 'pen', was the Governor and this is presumably why this term is part of the title of the Bank. The Governor, a term which in early English meant protector, guide or keeper, was to watch over the investment and ensure its safety. Perhaps the widows and merchants who invested in the Bank projected the need for a paternal figure, to keep them safe in uncertain times, onto the Governor. Bear in mind that the Bank was a high-risk venture on a national scale. It is difficult from our vantage point to realize what an innovative and daring project this was. The myth of its inevitability, of its timelessness, belies the level of risk taken by the projectors and investors. William III could have lost the war with France and all the bets would have been off, and all the money lost. The Treasury may have 'stopped' payments to the Bank as they once did to the London Goldsmiths. The Directors could have absconded with huge amounts of money. All in all, the project required that people believe in it, and promised that this trust and their money would ensure the nation's successful pursuit of trade and war.

In theory, the subscribers took a very personal risk. If the Bank ever owed more than the equivalent of its capital (£1,200,000) 'except upon Parliament Funds', the debt was to 'lie against particular members' as if it had been 'contracted under their own seal'. But as Clapham notes, 'This limited the issue of sealed bills to the £1,200,000. It also gave the proprietors a limited liability.'[98] Later, there were other bills issued, not marked with the Bank's seal in the presence of the Governor, Deputy Governor or two of the Directors. These effectively became new money through the act of alchemy which produces fractional reserve banking, or lending more than you have in the hope that all your promises will not be called in at once.

Rival banks and lotteries in the offing, of which there were many, such as the Land Bank and the Bank based on Tickets of the Million Adventure, must have been a direct threat to the income of the Bank of England. Giuseppi in his history of the Bank of England notes:

> With the advantage of knowing what happened to these rival concerns, we can now see that they were of small account, but lacking that advantage the Court [of Directors] must have felt no small anxiety regarding their potential menace; and there was more than a suspicion that any success they did attain was at the Bank's expense. For example, in the early part of 1695, Godolphin and other prominent Whigs sold their holdings of Bank stock, and word forthwith went round that Godolphin had reinvested in the proceeds of the Orphan's Fund.[99]

The Bank had many enemies. It was unreservedly a Whig institution, a progressive project that the landed gentry saw as a threat to their power. The connection between Whigs, money and projectors is clear enough to their Tory opponents, one describing them in 1702 as 'Knaves … who living on Grants and Taxes, are the Off-springs of War and Confusion'.[100] Indeed, some of them supported another form of bank – land banks – which backed the value of their loans on the value of land, an idea supported by Defoe too. The goldsmiths saw the Bank as a threat to their long-standing private banking business based on precious metals. Parliament saw it as a threat to their power in that the King could become dependent on the Bank, rather than on Parliament, to grant funds for war. The East India Company continually sought to undermine the Bank, as a commercial competitor. It is clear that this was a high-risk project and it is a matter of wonder that it came into existence and managed to survive at all. Its fortune was largely outside its control, dependent on what happened on the oceans and in lands far away, on weather and strategy, in war and trade and in public sentiment. A reassuring figure was needed to personalize this level of risk and uncertainty, to convince the punters that all would be well.

This assurance is carried in the idea of a Governor in and of itself, and the first Governor appears to have been chosen to exemplify such characteristics. Sir John Houblon was an extremely successful merchant and a respected figure in the City. 'Besides being Governor of the Bank of England from 1694-7, he was Lord Mayor 1695-6, Master of the Grocer's Company in 1696 and Lord of the Admiralty 1694-9; he is fully deserving of Pepys' tribute to him as "industrious"'.[101] He built himself a house in Threadneedle Street, which served as his home and place of business. This later became the site of the Bank of England, where it remains to this day. The section where the Governor works is still known as 'the parlours', and the staff list of the Bank was until quite recently known as the 'house-list'. He was held in high regard by the other directors, as is testified by their gift to him of a silver tankard in 1696 inscribed: 'The Gift of the Directors of the Bank of England to Sir John Houblon, Governor, Mayor of London, in token of his great ability and strict uprightness at a time of extreme difficulty'.[102] Presumably, this difficulty was the founding of the Bank, and the telling of its story during the first two years.

A recent Governor, Sir Mervyn King, in the foreword to the

latest history of the Bank which covers the troubled economic period from 1950–79, underlines this attitude to the Bank and its legendarily cool-headed Governors:

> However, the Bank is at its best in adversity, and whatever private doubts might have been harboured, heroic deeds were done. Governor Cromer famously assembled $3,000 million of central bank credits to support sterling over the telephone on a single morning in 1964. Roy Bridge, the Head of Foreign exchange, set and sprang traps for the sterling bears. Sir Jasper Hollom, the Deputy Governor, almost singlehandedly saved the financial system in 1973: The vignette of Hollom taking a call from a Burma shareholder is priceless.[103]

There is a promise in both the Bank and *Moll* that, as another famous banker writes in the twentieth century, 'All shall be well, all manner of things shall be well'.[104] But a promise is just a promise. Defoe explores the nature of a promise in *The Compleat English Tradesman* (1726) pointing out, in much the same way as the philosopher Jacques Derrida will much later, that a promise is by its nature contingent.[105] The author of an unpaid bill could not, he argued, be said to lie. The market is unpredictable and the author cannot be held responsible for this uncertainty:

> To break a solemn promise is a kind of prevarication, that is certain … But the Tradesman's answer is this: all those promises ought to be taken as they are made, namely, with a contingent dependence upon the circumstances of trade, such as promises made by others who owe them money, or the supposition of a week's trade bringing in money by retail, as usual, both of which are liable to fail … It is objected to this, that then I should not make my promises absolute, but conditional: To this I say that the promises, as is above observ'd are really not absolute, but conditional in the very nature of them,

and are understood so when they are made, or else they that hear them do not understand them as all human appointments ought to be understood.

As Sandra Sherman observes, 'The passage argues that uncertainty in credit relations instantiates the inescapable randomness of things, that in the market (as in every setting) conditionality is normative ... Everyone and no one is responsible if the text is a fiction.'[106] The promise of the Bank, just like the promise of the novel, is a fiction, and only fools and dupes fail to realize this. It's something that we now seem to have forgotten.

Conclusion

Moll Flanders and the Bank of England are fictional enterprises, imaginative productions, projections with no guarantees. They both exploit and create a shift in the operation of the imagination which fosters speculation of all kinds. Intangible realities, necessarily inhabiting a space outside the times and spaces of agriculture or small-scale craft production are traded as commercial ventures. Such speculations suggest limitless possibilities for the projectors involved but they are based on nothing other than a joint agreement to believe, or to pretend to believe. This means that a certain level of deceit is required to realize the projections, and tricks such as persuading the punters, naming, and cloaking the projection in recognized authorities are employed. Both involve a promise which can never be fulfilled, for it is the promise which is for sale. Both seek to manage anxiety and uncertainty in a world which is changing with dizzying speed. The next chapter outlines the revolutionary possibilities of this new space of composition and the ways in which these new possibilities are inherited by the novel and the organization.

3

Revolutions

The Projecting Age described in the previous chapter created, and was enabled by, anxiety and uncertainty as widely understood assumptions about stability and value began to disintegrate in the face of new imaginative possibilities. This chapter focuses on the revolutionary potential of this new space of composition. It seems to us that the Bank of England and *Moll Flanders* emerge in an age of revolution, an age when the foundations of value were becoming insecure. Both confront the same problems in challenging the traditional power structures of the seventeenth century and solve these problems in very similar ways in order to invent grounds which can provide them with authority. We will show that they are both early modern commercial institutions dependent on a wide and relatively democratized market for their success. Indeed, the market for both is shown to overlap, suggesting that they were shaped by the same forces. The chapter concludes by exploring the reactionary discourse which emerged to counter the power and authority of the Bank and the novel, a discourse which we think still shapes understandings of commercial organizations and the novel to this day.

Crowds and power

This was a revolutionary time. The Glorious Revolution of 1688 has tended to be approached as a rather civilized affair, a thoroughly English, well-mannered defense of justice and religious toleration. This view is largely based on the account given by the nineteenth-century historian and Whig politician, Thomas Babington Macaulay (1800–1859), in his hugely popular *History of England* (1855). The Yale historian Steve Pincus has challenged this account. The latter's *1688 The First Modern Revolution* overturns this 'old narrative' which 'emphasized the Revolution of 1688-89 as a great moment in which the English defended their unique way of life' and advances the argument 'that the English revolutionaries created a new kind of modern state. It was that new state that has proved so influential in shaping the modern world.'[107] Financial historians too, such as P.G.M. Dickson and Joel Mokyr,[108] have suggested that this period was revolutionary, and key to the financial developments of the modern period.

Of course there is fierce debate amongst academic historians regarding the technical definition of a revolution. We are using the term here as it is defined by Pincus:

> Revolutions thus constitute a structural and ideological break from the previous regime. They entail changes to both the political and socio-economic structures of a polity. They involve an often violent popular movement to overturn the previous regime. Revolutions change the political leadership and the policy orientations of the state. And revolutionary regimes bring with them a new conception of time, a notion that they are beginning a new epoch in the history of the state and its society.[109]

This revolution was political, social and economic and, on all three dimensions, challenged an elite group in favor of spreading power downwards – though not to the masses – and widening participation by redefining the state and the individual's relation to it. This was a period in which memories of ten years of civil war were still vivid. Traditional sources of authority, such as the monarchy and the Church, had been challenged, and close to 200 thousand people had been killed, out of a population of five million. The execution of Charles I in 1649 somewhat conclusively challenged the divine right of Kings, and ushered in the republicanism of Cromwell. The power of parliament grew. In 1660, the English, rather apologetically, restored the monarchy, crowning Charles II king. But the genie was out of the bottle. Authority could no longer be seen as 'invested' in a person by God but was understood to have been created, or at least given, by some version of 'the people'. Thus when the Catholic James II succeeded Charles and began to modernize the state, centralizing power, the English organized a rebellion. The protestant William III from Holland and his English wife, Mary II, took the throne. England became part of Dutch history, constantly at war with France over control of Europe and the Americas.

In all this, the power base was shifting from the monarchy and aristocracy to a growing middle class generally represented by the merchant Whigs. This is of course a simplification. Many merchant projects were dependent upon the investments of the traditional landed gentry, and many successful merchants purchased land in order to become members of the landed gentry. Indeed, the existence of anything that we might define as a middle class at this time has been questioned.[110] Joel Mokyr comments: 'As a conscious political entity, or even an organizing concept of cultural identity, the middle-class may well be a disreputable category in eighteenth century Britain. But the eighteenth century writers (such as Daniel Defoe and David Hume) who identified it knew of which they spoke when they referred to "the middling sort"'.[111] He later defines this middle class, citing Doepke and Zillibetti, as 'people with a different mentality, one of acquisitiveness, a desire for social upward mobility, and a willingness to invest in the education and well-being of their children'.[112] The emergence of a middling sort is exemplified by Defoe himself who, born straightforward Foe, changed his name to the grander-sounding Defoe and had a coat of arms created for his carriage. He earned his living from various entrepreneurial activities, and then later from a new profession: journalism, which was itself enabled by new technologies in print and publishing, and the spread of reading amongst the middling sort.

Although Pincus documents widespread support in the provinces, the epicenter of the revolution was London. London was growing in size and importance; people crowded into the city in search of new, more prosperous lives, many of them the poor and destitute who had been driven from the land by enclosures. There had been an increase in the population from 375,000 in 1650 to over 600,000 in 1700.[113] This rapid influx of people from the country had overwhelmed the space and produced a new dense and complex set of social relations. People who previously had a clear identity and role in their village frequently found themselves unknown and uprooted in a violent and socially divided city. In his biography of London, Peter Ackroyd describes this situation as Mobocracy:

> The salient fact was that London had grown immeasurably larger in the sixteenth and seventeenth centuries, and so obviously the size of its crowds was enlarged. In an atmosphere of religious and political controversy, too, there was no model of civic polity to restrain them.[114]

The sheer number of people crowded into one city led to an unusual mingling of classes in proximity, if not in understanding. By the early eighteenth century, there was a common perception that London was rife with criminality, and broadsides, pamphlet accounts of lives, as well as publications like *The Ordinary of Newgate, His Account,* and the *Old Bailey Sessions Papers* fed a public seemingly fascinated by the salacious details of any crime. It seems to be at this point that the scale and labyrinthine geography of the city begins to create a situation in which the strange and the wild can jostle shoulder-to-shoulder with civilization. As the novelist and magistrate Henry Fielding wrote in 1751:

Whoever indeed considers the cities of London and Westminster with the late vast addition of their suburbs, the great irregularity of their buildings, the immense number of lanes, alleys, courts and bye-places; must think that, had they been intended for the very purpose of concealment, they could scarce have been better contrived. Upon such a view, the whole appears as a vast wood or forest, in which such a thief may harbour with as great security, as wild beasts do in the deserts of Africa or Arabia.[115]

Casanova, after a visit to London in 1746, expresses horror at the breakdown of order he witnessed: 'In this chaos', he asserts, 'the flower of the nobility mingling in confusion with the vilest populace ... the common people affect to show their independence'.[116] In accounts of the time, we are presented with an unruly mob disciplined by the looming images of the army and the gallows, dying on 'Albion's fatal tree' [117] whilst the crowds bay their approval, or howl in protest. These are the crowded streets where Moll, a girl from a small town attracted to the wealth of London, pickpockets. The institutions by which she is contained and punished, though they never know her real name, are the Old Bailey and Newgate. *Moll Flanders* and the Bank of England emerge from and help to create this revolutionary space.

Revolutions, books and banks

The emergence of the novel reflects a shift in power away from a small elite to a wider middling sort. This was a move from various forms of patronage to a market. As Defoe sits down to write *Moll*, the relationship between himself as a writer and the audience is shifting. He had written for large audiences before in newspapers and pamphlets but this earlier writing generally had a message to communicate or an incident to recount that shaped the imaginative space between author and reader. He now has the experience of *Robinson Crusoe* behind him. The scale of the success of this book had taken everyone by surprise, hence the many hurried reprints of the text and the very many fraudulent copies, abridgements, chap books, ballads and sequels. Indeed, it had gone into four authorized editions between 25th April 1719 and 7th August of the same year. An unauthorized abridgement was published in the same August and it was serialized in a London newspaper from October onwards.[118] The same torrent of plagiarism follows, with the text of *Moll* being borrowed, edited, extended and copied in every format imaginable. Defoe now recognizes the market, an audience stretching even to the continent, and declares: 'Preaching of sermons is speaking to a few of mankind: printing of books is talking to the whole world'.[119] Power is shifting from the few to the many as arbiters of success and this inevitably opens up possibilities for literature, and for writers. As Johnson concludes later in the century: 'We have done with patronage ... An author leaves the great and applies to the multitude.'[120]

This is a qualitatively different experience and one which has a transformative effect on the possibilities of writing. It means for example, that Defoe can use ordinary language, the language of the people, of the street, of the *demos*. It means that the characters in his novel can be drawn from the ordinary people, from those around him. So rather than talking of Kings and Queens, nobles and ladies, he can take as his protagonist Moll Flanders, born a nobody. It means that his story does not have to be a rewrite of a mythical or classical tale but can be a credible plot which could have happened in the London that Defoe and his readers knew. These are the characteristics most often identified as the key components of this new genre, the novel.[121] It is, we argue, a particularly democratic moment, one in which new spaces were opening to outsiders, and particularly for people with projects. Defoe, an outsider to the establishment and therefore not sharing its landed but limited horizons, writes for a large, unaffiliated audience 'out there'. These much broader parameters shape the possible space of composition and hence the story. The philosopher Jacques Derrida claims in his essay 'This Strange Institution called Literature' that Literature as we know it begins in the late seventeenth century, and 'is linked to an authorization to say everything, and doubtless too to the coming about of the modern idea of democracy'. It seems to us that *Moll Flanders* can be seen as one of the moments in that 'beginning'. Derrida goes on to say that this modern Literature does not 'depend on a democracy in place, but it seems inseparable to me from what calls forth a democracy, in the most open (and doubtless itself to come) sense of democracy'.[122]

So the novel carries this democratic moment within its form – it is written by all kinds of people, for all kinds of people, about any type of subject, and can take place anywhere. Marthe Robert underlines this aspect of the form of the novel in an attempt to define the genre:

> The modern novel, whether it was born with Don Quixote's memorable escapade or on Robinson Crusoe's desert isle, and notwithstanding the distinguished and historically acknowledged ancestry it claims, is a newcomer to the literary scene, a commoner made good who will always stand out as something of an upstart, even a bit of a swindler, among the established genres it is gradually supplanting.[123]

Terry Eagleton, a Marxist literary critic, also notes the use of common language and people in the novel, and sees even its twentieth-century form as radical. He points out that 'Auerbach, a Jewish refugee from Hitler, was writing about the novel while in exile in Istanbul at the same time as Bakhtin was writing about it as a dissident in Stalinist Russia; and both men saw in it a populist strike against autocratic power'.[124] The novel created, and creates, new possibilities.

Politically speaking, this is known as democracy. We are set free from being mere functions of the grammar of God. It is we who give form and meaning to reality, and the novel is a model of this creative act. As the novel configures a new world into existence, in a profane parody of God's creation, so each individual shapes his or her inimitable life-history.[125]

By extension, then, Moll is a democratic figure, telling and shaping her own life history. She is an orphan born in Newgate who refuses her place in society and decides to become a gentle-woman. She feeds off a middle-class family, plays the market for husbands, and thieves from those 'above her'. She does all this with style and panache until she does indeed make herself a respectable gentlewoman with financial security and a reputation as a true penitent. As many commentators have observed, not only does Moll take control of her destiny in the story, it is as if she takes control of the story. Moll appears to escape Defoe, in that she gets away with everything despite the promise in the Preface that this will be a morality tale with the sinners punished and the good rewarded. Not only does Moll end up rich but there is little or no sense that she feels that her character has been permanently stained. She is penitent, or claims to be, and hence remains a gentlewoman according to her own account. It is a success story, whatever the 'pen' suggested at the start.

The Bank of England responds to and creates the same revolutionary principles. Its emergence challenges an elite in favor of a wider power base, 'the market', and it feeds and responds to the idea that the individual can create their own future. Pincus places the Bank of England at the heart of this revolutionary period, asserting that 'The creation of the Bank of England, war against France, and religious tolerance were all explicit goals of many of the revolutionaries'.[126] As we noted, the Bank was a Whig institution, competing for funds and status against the Tory-backed East India Company. Indeed, it was not until the Bank of England was established in 1694 that the new Whig regime could consider itself in some way part of the establishment at all. Dickson is unequivocal on the importance of the Bank to this revolution:

> Alliances were therefore important, they were almost certainly more important than other causes of English superiority alleged at the time and since, ranging from supposedly greater English naval and military skill through the virtues of Protestantism to the merits of roast beef and leather shoes, in ascending order of implausibility. More important even than alliances, however, was the system of public borrowing developed in the first half of the period (1689-1713), which enabled England to spend on war out of all proportion to its tax revenue.[127]

Similarly H.V. Bowen observes that although the respective significance of the Financial and Industrial revolutions will remain a matter for debate and controversy, 'there can be no denying the crucial role played by the Bank of England in allowing the state to mobilise and deploy financial resources on a global scale'.[128]

The Bank was revolutionary in its effect on the state's capacity to wage war but it was also radical in social terms. The emerging Bank spread power from a small elite, a land-owning group, to a wider base. Paterson himself reports that the idea of a Bank was itself seen as a revolutionary idea, even one likely to usher in a republic because it would be emulating Holland and the Bank of Amsterdam:

> Some of the Race, have been abroad in some Country or other, and in all their Peregrinations they never met with BANKS nor STORKS anywhere but only in Republicks. And if we let them set footing in England, we shall certainly be in danger of a Common-wealth ... Some said it was a new thing and they

did not understand it, besides they expected an immediate peace and so there would be no occasion for it. Others said this project came from Holland and therefore they would not hear of it, since we had too many Dutch things already.[129]

Banks were seen as dangerous by some sections of the population because they created a power base that was distinct from the king and parliament. The Bank of England wished to go even further and become a bank of issue, thereby encroaching on that most jealously guarded function of state, the money supply and coinage supplied by the Royal Mint. In this it was going further than other banks. One of the founders and first directors of the Bank, Sir Theodore Jansen, noted in his *Discourse concerning Banks* (1697) that he knew of about 25 banks in Europe, and that the Bank of England was unique amongst them in 'giving out Notes payable to Bearer'.[130] Jansen goes on to confirm that the Bank could not function without this ability to issue notes, a view which Sir John Clapham suggests

was evidently shared by his colleagues, though they covered up their opinion so well that one could read the clauses of the Act of Parliament to which the Bank owed its existence, or the whole of its Charter, without realizing that a new and experimental type of public bank was being created, a bank "for Conveniency" and "Income", and issue; but in the first place issue.[131]

As we have already seen, this was entirely deliberate. Paterson's initial proposal for the Bank put forward in 1691 was straightforward. He proposed to raise money 'upon a Fund of perpetual interest' instead of doing so by a loan for a fixed period. The capital was not to be repaid, the investors were buying the debt for the perpetual interest it would provide. The proposal would establish the idea of the national debt with which we are now familiar. In his initial proposal Paterson thought he could raise £1,000,000 at a charge to the state of £65,000 per year, or 6 per cent on the capital, plus £5,000 for managing the fund. He suggested that the subscribers be Trustees and that 'their Bills of Property should be current' so that the Bank could exchange the bills 'the better to give credit thereto and make the said Bills the better to circulate'. Clapham notes that 'the meaning of the words is not exactly clear; but the intention of setting up a bank of issue is clear enough'.[132] This was too radical. The Committee established to review government finances rejected the notion that the Bank would be able to issue circulating bills and the proposal was dropped. When Paterson put forward the proposal again in 1694, he had taken out any direct reference to a bank at all.

The Bank of England was surreptitiously established as an independent corporation, obliged to the King and government but not owned by them, and instead owned by its subscribers. The establishment of the Bank empowered a third source of wealth and power, separate from land and nobility. The original charter is a surprisingly egalitarian document, declaring that the subscription would be open to all, 'Natives and Foreigners, Bodies Politick and Corporate'.[133] There were to be 24 Directors who would form the Court of the Bank and they would be elected by those subscribers with over £500 invested. Each Director had to have his own money in the new Bank and the Governor could only serve for two years. The Directors swore upon election that they would be 'indifferent and equall to all manner of persons' and that they would give their best advice and assistance for the support and good government of the corporation'.[134] In the event, the Directors were drawn from a much smaller circle, largely the growing merchant classes of London. For example, Houblon was also Lord Mayor of London, and a number of his extended family also served as Directors. Despite the narrow circle, it is important to note that these were not men from old families, but of new wealth represented by an urban bourgeoisie, the *nouveau riche*. Paterson always claimed that 'the first framers and proposers of the Bank were only particular men, and not in public places or preferments'.[135]

These particular men were, however, most definitely protestant. As Giuseppi notes, the Directors were 'solid in their support of the "Glorious Revolution", protestants to a man'.[136] The Bank historian W. Marston Acres similarly presents the Bank as a 'stronghold of the Whigs and a bulwark of the protestant succession'.[137] Paterson himself was a covenanter, a type of Presbyterian dissenter who from the late sixteenth century onwards refused to accept the authority of the Bishops in Scotland. Defoe was a dissenter too, of course, and his novels are protestant in spirit, placing the individual as interpreter of their own destiny and not a pawn of authorities earthly or celestial.

The Bank and the novel depended on a commercial market for their success, a market which to some extent liberated the participants from patronage and created the potential for new power relationships. The next section explores the market for each and finds that they significantly overlap.

Commerce

Moll Flanders and the Bank are commercial enterprises. They each must answer to the needs, demands and desires of an emerging market, a population that wants to borrow, spend and read. In this respect, this new market could be imagined to be projecting the novel and the Bank, as the market's emerging needs and desires shape both.

Moll is shaped by the audience and by the bookseller mediating for that audience by imagining what they would buy. As far as can be ascertained, Defoe is paid by the page for *Moll* and this appears to have been a common arrangement, hence the familiar accusation in the early eighteenth century that writers produced as many pages as possible for economic reasons. This accusation was levelled at Defoe by an anonymous editor of the 1738 edition of *The Complete English Tradesman*. He concluded that Defoe's writing was generally 'too verbose and circumlo- cutory' and that 'to have a complete work come off his hands, it was necessary to give him so much per sheet to write it in his own way; and half as much afterwards to lop off its excres- cences'.[138] *Moll* was initially published as a full novel in January 1722, but David Shaw has discovered that there is now evidence that it was serialized shortly afterwards, probably beginning late March 1722, in at least two newspapers, *The London Post* and the *Kentish Post*.[139] The extracts from *Moll* appear on the first two pages of the newspapers suggesting that they were something significant, and hence that the publishers were using the serial- ization to attract new readers and retain the loyalty of existing ones. The extracts were also printed in such a way that they could easily be bound together to make up the full novel.

Paula R. Backscheider surmises that 'Defoe usually got a little money for editions after the first, and he may even have received a few guineas for the serialization'.[140] *Moll* the novel was as much an economic enterprise as Moll the character with speed and sleight of hand meaning money for both. Whatever the exact commercial arrangements, Backscheider notes that Defoe seems to have been living relatively well at this time. He was respon- sible for thousands of pages of print in 1722, *Moll* being followed by *Journal of the Plague Year*, the conduct manual *Religious Courtship*, as well as *The History and Remarkable Life of the Truly Honourable Col. Jacque*. This certainly suggests support for Watt's suggestion that Defoe was writing at such speed that he made mistakes, forgetting what he had written earlier and producing inconsistencies in the plot.[141] It is reasonable to assume that the commercial arrangement influenced the style and form of the novel. Being paid by the page meant that Defoe needed to write as quickly as possible, hence covering as many pages as possible and without revision. The text has this sense of rushing headlong from one event to the next, and sometimes jumping months or even years in a paragraph. The following is a representative single sentence, a breathless tumble of words:

> I was now as above, left loose to the World, and being still Young and Handsome, as every body said of me, and I assure you, I thought my self so, and with a tolerable Fortune in my Pocket, I put no small value upon myself: I was courted by several very considerable Tradesmen; and particularly, very warmly by one, a Linnen-Draper, at whose house after my Husband's Death I took a Lodging, his Sister being my Acquaintance; here I had all the Liberty, and all the Opportunity to be gay, and appear in Company that I could desire; my Landlord's Sister being one of the Maddest, Gayest things alive, and not so much Mistress of her Vertue, as I thought at first she had been: She brought me into a World of wild Company, and even brought home several persons, such as she lik'd well enough to Gratifie, to see her pretty Widow, so she was pleas'd to call me, and that Name I got a little time in Publick; now as Fame and Fools make an Assembly, I was here wonderfully Caress'd; had abundance of Admirers, and such as call'd themselves Lovers; but I found not one fair Proposal among them all; as for their common Design, that I understood too well to be drawn into any more Snares of that Kind: The case was alter'd with me, I had Money in my Pocket, and had nothing to say to them: I had been trick'd once by that Cheat call'd LOVE, but the Game was over; I was resolv'd now to be Married, or Nothing, and to be well Married, or not at all.[142]

Defoe seems to have some trouble actually coming to an end, not only of a sentence but ultimately of the entire novel itself. Indeed, Moll's concluding paragraphs seem to rush the story to a close in a fairly arbitrary manner. She could clearly have gone on.

The process of publication also influenced the text. Adrian Johns in *The Nature of the Book* has documented the complexity and unreliability of the publishing process.[143] It involved a number of stages and people: booksellers, printers, editors, apprentices, household members, and took place on several sites. Each person could and did interfere with the text, changing, amending and cutting to fulfil his or her own requirements and preferences. A note on the publication of *Moll* in the introduction to the 1971 Oxford Classics edition by G.A. Starr illustrates the problems. *Moll* was first published in January 1722. Six months later a second, 'corrected' edition appeared. Starr concludes that:

> compression seems to have been the chief objective in revising. This is to say that economic considerations on the part of the publishers, rather than aesthetic considerations on Defoe's part, probably dictated the preparation of a 'Corrected' second edition: by reducing 27 ½ octavo gatherings to 24 ½, enough was presumably saved in paper-costs to offset the expense of completely resetting the type, and of engaging someone other than the compositor to prune the text. Much of the compression, however, is clearly the work of the compositor, who has chosen smaller type for the preface, run paragraphs together, and used other space-saving devices. The crucial question is whether Defoe was responsible for altering the text itself: in my opinion he probably had no hand in the revisions.[144]

The size and shape of *Moll* was clearly sculpted by the publishing process, which in turn was influenced by a publisher's estimate of what they might sell, and hence what they might earn. Defoe's authorship matters, but the text was clearly shaped by the economics of writing, the problems with copyright and typesetting, and even the price of paper. 'The Author' was only one of the elements in the process that brought the commodity to market.

More self-evidently, the Bank was an economic enterprise. Paterson personally invested £2,400 in the Bank and expected to make money. Withdrawing a year later, he argued that he should be recompensed for his efforts in establishing the Bank. In 1718, after petitioning Parliament regarding his part in the disastrous attempt to found a colony on the Gulf of Darien in what is now Panama, he did eventually receive £16,754 from Queen Anne for 'service to his country'.[145] As well as personal benefit, Paterson appeared to want to establish the Bank for national commercial reasons, hoping to encourage trade – as we might expect from a member of the mercantile classes. He also seems to have recognized the importance of providing a reliable source of credit, backed by the state, as is clearly outlined in the opening paragraph of his 'Brief Account of the Intended Bank of England':

> The want of a Bank, or publick Fund, for the convenience and security of great Payments, and the better to facilitate the circulation of Money, in and about this great and opulent City, hath in our time, among other Inconveniences, occasion'd much unnecessary Credit, to the loss of several Millions, by which Trade hath been exceedingly discourag'd and obstructed.[146]

Money had been held or loaned on trust before the Bank was established, the trust largely being associated with the honorable name of the people directly involved. The Bank turned these trust and risk relations into a business in much the same way as Moll, as both character and novel, turned her relationships into business transactions with financial benefits clearly catalogued.

Markets

Was the market the same for the novel and the Bank? Were they constituted from the same projected audience? It has generally been asserted that the Bank and the novel emerged in response to a growth of the middling sort, and of the gradual displacement of feudal assumptions about entitlement and power. However, there is now evidence to suggest that the audience for both investment and novels was much wider than we might assume, and that it overlapped significantly.

Pincus has completed an examination of the initial list of subscribers to the Bank and confirms that it was very definitely a Whig institution. The subscribers were supporters of Protestantism, William III and the revolution which displaces an older order. A review of the initial subscribers now published on the Bank of England website reveals a much wider spread of 'quality' than previously recognized, including drapers, soapmakers, Blacksmiths, spinsters and widows. Recent research by Ann M. Carlos and Larry Neal also suggests a much wider market for investments than generally assumed:

> The Transfer Ledgers record roughly 7,000 transfers during 1720, while the Ledger Books from 1720-25 record over 8,000 individuals holding stock. The analysis finds the customer base had breadth and depth, comprising individuals from across the social spectrum, from all over England and Europe. The market was diverse and liquid. Activity during the Bubble came from those living in and around London, with most traders participating in the market only twice at most. While the majority of participants were men, there was a sizeable female presence. Men as a group lost money from their market activity, but women made money.[147]

A similar development has taken place in our understanding of the market for the novel. There has been a prevailing assumption, usually derived from discussions about the novel from the early eighteenth century, that the majority of the consumers of the novel were women, and that the reading of novels was part of the growth of a bourgeois leisured class. A cornerstone of Watt's argument in regard to the rise of the novel is a marked growth in the size of the reading public around the turn of the century. However, he goes on to question the actual scale of the increase.

> The only contemporary estimate of the size of the reading public was made very late in the eighteenth century: Burke estimated it at 80,000 in the nineties. This is small indeed, out of a population of at least six millions; and would probably imply an even smaller figure for the earlier part of the century with which we are most concerned.[148]

If we take 60,000 as a generous estimate of literacy in 1704 and assume that less than half of the literate group were women, then the reading public these books were aiming at would be very small. Consequently, it is likely that far more men read prose than is acknowledged. Indeed, we do know that some men did read prose fiction as they discuss it in their writing. Pope, Swift and Johnson for example all refer to reading novels. We also know that some men read fiction in secret, as Samuel Pepys records of himself in his diary.[149] Novak cites evidence to suggest that 'despite attempts to disparage his work, Defoe was always read by an audience that spanned the spectrum of the reading population', including men.[150]

A developing interest in the history of readers has led to investigations which shed doubt on the idea that novels were written for a limited market of women. Ian Jackson documents evidence which suggests a much wider readership of books in general and of fiction in particular:

> The records of the Clays, booksellers of the east Midlands, have been studied in depth by Jan Fergus. Such evidence casts serious doubt on many received ideas about eighteenth century readerships: Fergus finds that among the Clays'

customers in the East Midlands, at least, far more women read magazines than read fiction, a genre more conventionally associated with female readers in contemporary and subsequent commentary. Men, as well as women, borrowed sentimental fiction from the Clays' Warwick circulating library, and provincial servants chose much the same reading material as their employers.[151]

There have always been some unresolved issues in assumptions about the market for the novel. On the one hand the market is described as targeting leisured women and on the other, the less cultured elements among the literate. However, it seems likely that novels were read by a much larger market than either of these descriptions suggest. The fact that *Moll* was serialized in a newspaper as a front-page lead indicates a wide audience, including men. Of course literacy levels were still low and many people could not afford books. Watt points out that *Robinson Crusoe* cost 5 shillings when a skilled journeyman's wage was roughly £1 per week. No wonder then that a few novels like *Crusoe* and, we now know, *Moll* were serialized in newspapers which cost around 1p, a far more affordable price.[152] As a result, we might surmise that the original *Moll*, as well as all the ballads, abridgements and plagiarisms, were read by a wider spread of the population than might previously have been assumed, including both the gentry and a growing number of people from the middling sort.

The subscribers to the Bank were originally thought to represent a rarified section of the population. Our suggestion is that both would have been comprised of a much wider market, centered in and around London but spreading far afield. This means that it is highly likely that the people who purchased the novels and the people who subscribed to Banks and lotteries involved a huge overlap who did both. The Bank and *Moll* were shaped by this evolving market and its much more inclusive social mix. This was a new sort of public, and any discussion of the growth of this market must also include a consideration of the impact of the coffee-houses and the culture of social exchange that they promoted.

Coffee-houses

The coffee-houses had a significant effect on the emergence of the Bank and the novel. There were an estimated 3000 in London at the end of the seventeenth century, and an anonymous and rather defensive pamphlet (*Coffee-Houses Vindicated*) described them as 'The sanctuary of health, the nursery of temperance, the delight of frugality, an academy of civility, and a free-school of ingenuity'. People who would not perhaps have come across each other in the socially restrictive institutions of the earlier seventeenth century met here, discussed matters, literary, political and economic, and sometimes formed alliances. This was a space which encouraged a market in ideas, a counterpoint to the marketplace of people and things found on the city streets. Pincus summarizes the situation:

> English coffee-houses were novel institutions in the later seventeenth century. Within a few decades every English village or market town with any pretensions had its own coffee-house. Although each coffee-house must have had its own particular charm, by and large English coffee-houses all shared the same cultural characteristics. They were venues where locals could come to exchange news, read the most recent newspapers and pamphlets, and conduct business. The coffee-house was an institution ideally suited to a society experiencing rapid urbanization and commercialization.[153]

The historian G.M. Trevelyan observes that 'At the coffee house you could see blue ribbons and stars sitting familiarly with private gentlemen as if they had left their quality and degrees of distance at home'.[154] We know that Paterson frequented coffee-houses. His second wife, Hannah Kemp, appears to have been the manager of one.[155] It is in the coffee-houses that Paterson is likely to have come across some of his co-projectors, men such as Sir John Trenchard, who joined him in the project to establish a water supply for London from the ponds at Hampstead Heath. Paterson was awarded maiden shares in this venture, which signals that he was an initiator of the project. It is in the coffee-houses that the pros and cons of a bank would have been debated, perhaps inspired by merchants from the Levant and Holland describing the banks and commercial arrangements they had come across in their travels.

Paterson called his group to found a bank for England simply 'The Society' and recruited his old co-projector Sir William Phips (or Phipps) to the cause. In 1687, Paterson had invested in Phips' successful adventure which culminated in finding a Spanish galleon laden with £300,000 worth of treasure. Forrester observes that the 'arrival of the colourful figure of Phips in London must have helped. He had come as part of a delegation from Massachusetts seeking a new charter for the colony.'

> Phips was at first the only titled person Paterson could boast as a supporter. But on 21st October he made a breakthrough. At a meeting held in the Sun Tavern close by the Royal Exchange, six new recruits were accepted into 'The Society'. Among them were another two knights of the realm, one of them Sir John Houblon, a mighty merchant of London, and one of five merchant brothers. Houblon was to go on to become the first Governor of the Bank of England less than three years later.[156]

They met here regularly until the Bank was established. This 'society' must have been something of a motley crew with a Scots adventurer, a New England treasure hunter, as well as merchants and Lords. For his second proposal in 1694 Paterson managed to attract Montague and Godfrey. Paterson came across Lord Montague when he was called as chief witness before the Parliamentary Committee appointed to receive proposals for raising supplies for the navy. Montague was then one of the Commissioners of the Treasury.[157] In previous times, Paterson would have been unlikely to have socialized with someone like Montague, since they would not have moved in the same circles. This new civil 'society' is itself a reflection of that commingling of classes that Casanova describes, people with widely different backgrounds and occupations mixing together and then sometimes choosing to act in concert.

The public sphere which the social theorist Jurgen Habermas[158] explores as the basis for a new form of social order, and which grew from these coffee-houses, first seems to have developed through the discussion of literature. This doesn't mean that books and dramas were all that was discussed, as John Barrell points out in his article on 'Coffee-house Politicians'.[159] However, the coffee-house discussions seem to have fostered and reflected a delight in the novel, both as in the *new* and the news. J. Paul Hunter suggests that the novel form, 'with its distinctively modern and anti-aristocratic tendency to encompass the daily, the trivial, the common and the immediate', reflects the nature of the discussion and experience in the coffee-house. 'The early novelists', he declares, 'shared the same public taste for contemporaneity and novelty and quickly discovered how to blend it into a substantial and complex web of narrative and discursive prose, creating in effect a kind of portable coffee-house of elongated conversation in print'.[160] Coffee-houses facilitated the emergence of *Moll* and the Bank, and these forms inherit the conversational possibilities of the coffee-house. But it was not an easy ride because neither the Bank nor *Moll* went unchallenged. Revolutions have to be fought, they do not simply happen. There were reactionary forces aligned against the Bank and the novel, and we think that this battle established a way of thinking that still shapes contemporary understandings of books and organizations.

Reactions

Revolutions do not go unchallenged and the story of the 'Glorious' Revolution as a peaceful one – the 'restoration' of a previous order – is not borne out by events. Pincus has demonstrated that 1688 required the taking up of arms by ordinary people and that there was significant bloodshed. Violence did not occur in one pitched battle but spread throughout the country in hundreds of uprisings by 'the rabble', 'the mob' or 'the multitude' as they are figured in accounts of the time.[161] There are vivid accounts of London ablaze and the destruction of Churches and Chapels as the mob sought out priests and their political supporters.

Moll's ambitions for social mobility did not go unchallenged either. At eight years old Moll is told that she will need to go into service soon, that is to say, to become a servant. Moll becomes very distressed at the idea of service and her 'good motherly nurse' pacifies her by promising that she will try to prevent it until she is much older. 'Well', reports the narrator Moll, 'this did not Satisfie me, for to think of going into Service, was such a frightful Thing to me, that if she had assur'd me I should not have gone till I was 20 years old, it wou'd have been the same to me, I sho'd have cry'd, I believe all the time, with the very Apprehension of its being so at last'.[162] The nurse becomes angry and scornful: 'is the Girl mad?' she questions, 'would you be a gentlewoman?' When Moll responds that she does indeed wish to become a gentlewoman, the nurse roars with laughter and scorn, and goes on to imply (in ironic prediction) that the only gentlewoman Moll will be is a whore.

The same scornful tone, the suggestion that you should know your place, is echoed in some responses to the novel *Moll*

Flanders itself and to the novel as a literary form. The literary elite were dismissive of 'hack' writers such as Defoe, those who wrote for money, and worked on Grub Street. This was a rather Bohemian and poverty-stricken street in central London, known for a concentration of protestants, prostitutes and hacks. Those who wrote had traditionally been supported either by their own wealth or by wealthy patrons and thus were linked to some notion of public virtue and purpose which was seen to reside in the 'noble' aristocracy. The new breed of writers were not linked to anything but their bookseller and the popular audience, and so were regarded as dangerous to public virtue. Men of letters, those of the literary establishment such as Pope, Swift and Addison, were derisory about the aesthetic and moral values of these insurgents to Literature. The literary historian Brean Hammond[163] contends that the literati deliberately sought to establish a discourse that devalued the professionalization of writing or writing for money, as opposed to traditional notions of patronage from the aristocracy, while simultaneously constructing their own ways of profiting from the new market in publishing. Pope, for example, clearly articulated his position as an advocate of a conservative ideology. His long poem the *Dunciad* (published in different versions in 1728, 1729 and 1742) mocked professional writers, presenting them as uneducated dunces and inferior to those trained in the classics. The profit motive is presented as demeaning and as producing inferior art.

Hammond draws on the work of David Foxon to demonstrate that despite this overt position,[164] Pope, the son of a linen merchant himself, was in fact 'the first writer who owed his success entirely to the adroit manipulation of the publishing industry. Whereas Pope's writing has helped to shape a lasting distaste for profit as a motive in literature that the writer hopes will be considered of enduring value, he was himself profit's creature'.[165] Pope set up a subscription for his work amongst the upper classes. As Leslie Stephen notes, Pope's subscription technique meant that he 'received a kind of commission from the upper class' to produce his writing, and effected a break with past practice by replacing the individual patron with a 'kind of joint-stock body of collective patronage'.[166] His books were marketed to appeal to this group. Hammond sets out to show how the careers of minor and major writers at this time were influenced by how they positioned themselves in regard to this revolution in writing and publishing:

> Conservative reaction against and anxiety over proliferating print, and its apparent corollary declining literary standards, is an important determinant of satiric 'voice': yet study of the careers of writers like Dryden, Pope and Gay should reveal that the attempt to preserve writing as the enclave of anti-professional purity could only proceed by capitalizing on the energies that this stance affects to despise.[167]

Colin Nicholson makes a similar observation in *Writing and the Rise of Finance*. He notes that Swift, Pope, Gay – as well as their contemporaries John Arbuthnot, Henry St. John and Thomas Parnell Pope – railed against the dissenters, who represented the rise of the newly monied men, and in so doing inadvertently testified to 'the power of an insurgent ideology'. Nicholson goes on to expose their double dealing:

> While publicly opposing the rapidly expanding financial systems and institutions of his time, like his friends and colleagues Pope participated in them and profited from the opportunities they presented. So it becomes an interesting reflection upon subsequent literary canon-formation and the cultural valorisations it encodes that some of the most remembered voices from a time of the greatest explosion of commercial and financial activity England had hitherto seen, publicly set themselves at variance with what was happening

while privately seeking profit from it … The installation of modern structures of finance and investment and the shifting configurations of power they represented and entailed were vigorously contested by the writers who famously grouped themselves around Bolingbroke, initially in the Brothers Club founded in the summer of 1711. Swift was a member from the beginning; Pope and Gay soon joined. Out of the Brothers Club grew the Scriblerus Club, and from there came their capital satires *Gulliver's Travels*, *The Beggar's Opera*, and the *Dunciad*.[168]

The attacks on *Moll* and Defoe were vigorous and vicious. *Moll Flanders* was dismissed as being intended only for the lower orders and uneducated readers[169] and Defoe himself appears as one of the dunces in *The Dunciad*. There was double dealing on both sides. In the late 1720s Defoe had publically railed against the dangerous influence of Gay's *Beggar's Opera* even as he sought to sell his books on pirates and thieves. Indeed, he wrote two best-selling pamphlets in 1724 in which the housebreaker Jack Sheppard became a clever jester, an account darkly reprised by Gay in the figure of his character Macheath. In an anonymous tract published in 1720 – *The Battle of the Authors Lately Fought in Covent-Garden, between Sir John Edgar, generalissimo on one Side, and Horatio Truewit on the Other* – Defoe is made to speak as the epitome of ignorance:

> I take it Great Goddess, that ignorance here is the chief Claim, and in that I think I have as great a Right as any Author, this Nation ever beheld: let me add, that my Ignorance has found the greatest Success, Hundreds of Volumes have I printed, both in Prose and Rhime, which have been greedily swallow'd, not only in England, Scotland and Ireland, but even as far as the East and West-Indies: The gentleman who spoke last indeed has had good Luck in some Penny Papers,

but when did he venture upon such volumes as Jure Divino, and Robinson Crusoe? Which my very Enemies own to be extraordinary Triumphs of Ignorance, there is still this difference between the Knight and myself that he seems to deserve a Suspicion of some knowledge ... whereas, I without either Free-school or House Learning, started from my Stocking-Shop, and in a thrice became a Voluminous, and taking Author.[170]

Such accusations of lack of learning might have stung, but Defoe defended his 'ignorance' in his posthumously published *The Compleat English Gentleman* with an attack on 'meer' (that is to say 'proper' or 'pure') scholars.

I think our meer scholars are a kind of mechanicks in the schools, for they deal in words and syllables as haberdashers deal in small ware. They trade in measure, quantityes, dactyls, and spondaes, as instrument-makers do in quadrants, rules, squares, and compasses; etymologyes, and derivations, prepositions and terminations, points, commas, colons and semi-colons, etc. are the product of their brain, just as gods and devils are made in Italy by every carver and painter; and they fix them in their proper stations in perspective, just as they do in nitches and glass windows.[171]

This was a class war. The aristocratic nobility were losing power to the merchants and the mobs, the classics to the commoners, and the 'monied men' of the Bank are lumped in with 'hack' writers of the novel in the reactionary movement against the revolution.

When all else fails, call them women. A further way of demeaning their enemies was to characterize both the novel and the Bank as female in an attempt to emasculate them. Catherine Ingrassia examines this feminization with particular regard to Pope:

As Pope subsequently indicates in *Epistle to Bathurst* (1733) and the 1743 edition of the *Dunciad*, the commercialisation of literature and the growth of speculative investment, and the participants in each phenomenon, hacks and stockjobbers, were both for him symptomatic of a larger cultural problem. His representation of the intertwined activities of the literary and financial spheres emphasises what he regards as the absence of masculinity, indeed the feminisation of a new breed of economic, literary and political subject. Gendering the participants and their practices, Pope attempts to diminish them by highlighting the stereotypically feminised characteristics that he feels influenced their actions and the direction of culture as a whole.[172]

So those involved in the money markets were also represented as female in what appears to be a parallel process. Nicholson notes that the new financial forces were often depicted as fickle and mysterious. The people of the time, he says,

> encountered what we now term finance capitalism as a system of credit that expanded and shrank as developing stock and money markets rose and fell. Public Credit, sometimes perceivable as 'the business confidence' or 'market forces' of the time, seemed to them a most mysterious entity that would or would not manifest itself; appearing to possess a will of its own yet apparently open to coaxing into a participatory and enabling movement. As a way of negotiating and controlling this new agency, the representation of Credit as an inconstant, often self-willed but sometimes persuadable woman gained a certain cross-party currency. In literary texts already celebrated for their articulation with a public awareness of far-reaching changes in the organization of society, the rhetoric of Eve as fateful temptress survives in altered usage.[173]

This pattern of representation appears in numerous texts relating to both financial and literary activities. Liz Bellamy also draws out the connections made between the new financial forces, the novel and immorality, or the unleashing of uncontrollable female desires as dangerous:

> Other writers of early tracts invoked the language of morality, condemning luxury and effeminacy in order to buttress the case against consumption. The author of *Britannia languens: or, A Discourse of Trade* (1680) presents a catalogue of vice and debauchery that is liable to result from a consumptive trade, including drunkenness, idleness, 'promiscuous copulation' and 'claps and poxes'. This locates the danger of luxury firmly within the lower class and it reinforced the concept that the purpose of trade was to strengthen the nation, rather than to satisfy the greed of individuals, for since economic theory disavowed individual spending, the only justification for economic expansion was the consolidation of the interests of the state. Thus within these early works the interests of the public were identified with the interests of the state.[174]

Similarly, the historian J.G.A. Pocock asserts that economic man was perceived as a feminized version of a real man. He was an effeminate or emasculated being 'still wrestling with his own passions and hysterias and with anterior and exterior forces let loose by his fantasies and appetites'.[175]

Given this background, with both novel and market often articulated as feminine, uncontrolled and dangerous, Defoe's creation of *Moll* is an audacious act which seems to take the battle head on. It is almost as brave as his famous experience in the pillory as a punishment for publishing *The Shortest Way with the Dissenters* in 1702, a satirical attack upon the high clergy. Defoe could have expected a painful and ignominious event, to be pelted with rotten food or even bricks and to hang in the pillory defenseless. Instead he turned the event into a public triumph, challenging the mob to understand the politics of punishing those like him who dare to speak up against a privileged elite:

> Tell them 'twas because he was too bold,
> And told those Truths, which shou'd not ha' been told.
> Extoll the Justice of the land
> Who Punish what they will not understand.
> Tell them he stands Exalted there
> For speaking what we wou'd not hear:
> And yet he might ha' been secure,
> Had he said less, or wou'd he had said more.[176]

Novak comments that 'If it did not create a revolution, it helped preserve his life from the "Fury of the Street"'.[177] So when writing a novel to follow *Robin Crusoe*, far from flinching away from a feminine discourse, Defoe chooses to write about a woman, a whore no less, and to write in her voice, thus writing as if he is a woman himself. Yet even though the novel was attacked as being written merely for highly strung women, it is very likely that given the figures relating to sales and literacy, many readers were in fact men. Indeed, as mentioned earlier, Moll's voice seems to imply a male reader in its often knowing tone and in its salacious plot, and Moll leaves her children behind with a carelessness that might alarm a generally female audience. We might think of Defoe here as a man pretending to be a woman writing for an audience that is pretending not to read the novel while actually reading it in secret. Just as Swift and others invested in the new joint-stock companies in secret while publically deriding them, so does Moll's voice hide secrets, while claiming truth.

The Bank of England herself works this gendered imagery to advantage. The projectors used a female icon for the new Bank, Britannia, as discussed in chapter 2. She is seen as an emblem of

Britain, and as a strong woman who cannot be demeaned. The Bank later becomes known as 'The Old Lady of Threadneedle Street' and the house magazine is titled *The Old Lady* until 2007. No one can be sure when and how this nickname arose but it can be tracked as far back as 1797 when a cartoon by James Gilray depicted an old lady sitting on a chest full of gold, marked 'Bank of England', while being addressed by William Pitt, the younger. The cartoon is entitled 'Political Ravishment: or, The Old Lady of Threadneedle Street in Danger'. Giuseppi suggests that this cartoon may have been inspired by a speech made by Sheridan in the House of Commons in which he referred to 'an elderly lady in the City, of great credit and long standing who had ... unfortunately fallen into bad company'.[178] This image of the woman in charge of her credit, though in danger from her circumstances, very much parallels the narrative figure of Moll. Although, the unruly desires of the young woman in the novel are presumably under firm control in the figure of the elderly woman.

Moll and the Bank are resisted and compromised, as are all revolutions. We have already outlined the deceit and sleight of hand they required to come into being: the legerdemain and *deceptio visus* identified by Defoe in his *Essay upon Projects*. In addition, they each require a level of acceptance by established powers in order to be able to establish themselves. Thus King William is the initial subscriber to the Bank and the Bank is as dependent on the King as the King is on the Bank. So too is the author dependent on the good graces of the reader. Defoe puts a whore center-stage but then sets in motion an editing 'pen' to correct any inappropriate language and keep the reader safe from defilement by association:

... the original Story is put into new Words, and the Stile of the famous Lady we here speak of is a little alter'd, particularly she is made to tell her own Tale in modester Words than she told it at first; the Copy which first came to Hand, having been written in Language, more like one still in Newgate, than one grown penitent and Humble, as she afterwards pretends to be.[179]

By implication, the novel is not written *for* someone who is of the mob, and who shares their vulgar tastes. Rather it is written *about* the mob, and the properly decent reader can be assured that their morals are safe and unimpugned. Such careful positioning, of King and reader, shows that a certain acceptance and legitimacy was needed for both the Bank and *Moll* to be realized. They both had to be seen to be able to access some authority from established audiences, and hence to at least partly disguise their radical implications by pretending to be something else. Their success at doing this is shown (as McKeon suggests in regard to the novel[180]) by the fact that both were quickly accepted by the established powers of the gentry and the new mercantile classes.

Conclusion

The Bank and *Moll Flanders* were both part of a social, political and economic revolution. They both responded to and created this revolution, bringing a new market for investments and imaginations into existence which reflected the new distributions of money and power within the social order of the time. From this perspective they are both projected by a new sort of market, and must answer to the same demands and desires. This means that both used similar strategies to gain credibility, and were similarly contested by those who felt that they had something to lose, whether in terms of being class upstarts or gendered and inconstant. Their ultimate successes resulted in a reconfiguration of the powers and imagination of their age. We contend that they are both emancipatory in impetus, part of a modern revolution which produced the organized world that we now live in, and the creative genres and markets that allowed such a world to become possible. In the next chapter, we will open up those spaces a little more, by exploring just what it means for something imaginary – like a novel or an organization – to become 'real'.

4

Invisible Hands

The previous chapter told a story in which *Moll Flanders* and the Bank challenged traditional authority. They were both reflections of The Glorious Revolution, and of a wider revolution that involved a shift in the understanding of the nature of truth, a shift from the divine to the empirical, from the assumed to the demonstrated. The world, and the role of power within it, was to be understood through the senses and through reason. This chapter argues that a valorization of the empirical translated into a valuing of the autonomous and the impersonal; 'objectivity' became a criterion of truth. *Moll Flanders* and the Bank are both presented as true, and so worthy of credit, by virtue of being presented as self-moving objects. They become 'things' in themselves, not contingent outcomes of particular social relations. They are seen as true to themselves, providing the conditions for establishing their own truth-telling, and so to be valued as objects.

We argue that these become necessary and primary conditions of both the novel and the organization, with far-reaching conse-quences. These requirements demand the death of the projector, or of the author.[181] The work, the product, begins to overshadow and even hide the agents who produced it. Who is then in control, and how is this projecting taking place? This chapter suggests that at key moments in the emergence of *Moll* and the Bank the accidental, or indeed even the supernatural, is required to keep the plot going. In both there is a kind of 'accidental inevitability' at work, a sense of a combination of chance and fate producing certain sorts of outcomes. Writers, both of fiction and economics, have often used the metaphor of 'an invisible hand' to describe this sense of a project being beyond the control of individuals. It's an uncanny metaphor for a truth that is invisible but strangely known, the result of collecting together many individual acts to compose something that then claims a life of its own.

Proving the empirical

A key argument in McKeon's search for the origins of the novel is that the late seventeenth century underwent an epistemological revolution which challenged the idea that truth was given by God and communicated through the hierarchies of church and monarchy. Truth was instead to be discovered by the use of the senses, through the observation and exploration of the natural world as it was presented to all who paid attention. Developments and discoveries in 'science', most commonly exemplified by the successes of Newton and the Royal Society, hence celebrated an empirical standard for truth claims. These developments were supported by a Protestant individualization of the nature of truth. This, for example, stressed the Bible as a document to be read and interpreted by each person in their own language, not a text with a 'real' meaning which could only be understood by certain categories of people. McKeon's sense of a revolution in ways of knowing at this time is profound. He asserts that what is most important about this revolution is 'that it entails a transformation from metaphysics and theology to epistemology'.[182] Truth was to be judged by objective criteria, not determined by popes and monarchs.

Moll declares itself from the opening page as a documentary object, separate from the author. The title assumes the existence of Moll as an already known and renowned character, proclaiming that this is an account of:

The Fortunes and Misfortunes of the Famous Moll Flanders,

& C.

Who was Born in NEWGATE

This opening denies that she is a creation of Defoe, asserting instead her own warrant to truth. Most significantly the text is 'Written from her own MEMORANDUMS'; that is, from an empirical object, complete and bounded, which was 'found' and then transcribed by a pen. This was to become a convention of the early English novel: an account would be found of a life, adventure, journey, diary, which would then be published for the world to see. Whether told in the corner of a public house, discovered in a book shop or sent to the author anonymously, this was part of the process of validating the story, of proving that it was true, because it was a true history 'found' by the author. The novel had to be separated from the author. McKeon points up the implications: 'From this perspective, the author who asserts the historical truth of his narrative validates it by alienating it from himself, thereby stamping it as a documentary object whose value depends upon its autonomy, its separability from himself'.[183] This autonomy becomes a fundamental principle of the novel, and the success of a particular fiction is then judged on whether it fulfills its own requirements as a work. Defoe pushes home the 'objective' nature of his story in the Preface, declaring it to be a 'private History'. Nonetheless, he says, he has had to alter some of the cruder language because 'the Copy which came first to Hand, having been written in a Language, more like one still in Newgate' was not suitable for publication. The truth of the account is even further emphasized with the customary method of redacting certain places and names – 'the town of S_____', or 'Lord _____' – as if this information were too sensitive to be released. Through such faking of fact, the story is presented as a complete, intact object; a true fiction whose truth is warranted by what everyone knows are really lies. Compare this to the Bank.

The Bank of England had to be created by Act of Parliament and by Royal Charter. As discussed earlier, it was presented as a method of gaining money to fund the war with France by raising taxes:

An Act for granting to their Majesties severall Rates and Duties upon Tunnage of Ships and Vessells and upon Beere Ale and other Liquors for secureing certain Recompenses and Advantages in the said Act mentioned to such persons as shall voluntarily advance the summe of Fifteene hundred thousand pounds towards carrying on the Warr against France.[184]

The Act goes on to turn 'such Persons' into a single body identified by the object of a common seal, declaring that it will 'incorporate all and every such Subscribers and Contributors theire ... Successors or Assignes to be one Body Corporate and Politick by the name of The Governor and Company of the Banke of England and by the same name of The Governor and Company of the Banke of England to have perpetuall succession and a Comon Seale'.[185] The techniques employed here to transmute an imaginary projection into some kind of object have been discussed earlier. It is a wonderful demonstration of the performative power of language to create things, and to turn many things into one. The key point for our purpose here is that the idea and the persons involved are turned into an autonomous object, independent of any particular person or people. This is language that does things, a form of magic or alchemy that makes something real by saying it. The Royal Charter establishes the Bank by making it 'hereby constituted':

And we do hereby for Us, our heirs and Successors, declare, limit, direct and appoint, that the aforesaid Sum of Twelve Hundred Thousand Pounds so subscribed as aforesaid, shall be, and be called, accepted, esteemed, reputed and taken, The Common Capital and Principal Stock of the Corporation hereby constituted...
By Writ of Privy Seal Pigott.[186]

The Bank is presented in this document as separate from all 'the persons' who make it or constitute it, and must be seen to be so in order to be true to the performance that it rests upon. We must behave as if the organization existed in order for the organization to exist, and the more robust the belief, the more stable the organization. This is a primary condition of the Bank of England's existence and one nicely reflected in a speech to celebrate the Bank's 300th anniversary in 1994 by the then Deputy Governor Rupert Pennant-Rea:

> Nobody who works for the Bank of England can fail to appreciate the contemporary value of its history. It is not a question of detailed knowledge: more a matter of sensing that an institution that has survived for 300 years must have some enduring raison d'etre, as good for the future as it has been for the past. The Bank was there, and is here; it is bigger than any of the individuals in it, and always has been.[187]

There is something rather relentless, almost insecure, about this demand. The idea that the organization comes before us and will be there after us, appears necessarily true but of course we know that there is no such thing as 'the Bank of England', apart from the people and buildings that we can see and touch now. And even the physical manifestations have changed, as people die and stone crumbles. Nonetheless, a sort of projected spectral reality is established as a necessary requirement of the organization. The Bank was organized as a joint-stock company following Paterson's 1690 model with the Hampstead Water Company, which supplied running water to London. The idea that the impersonal is true and objective is central to this idea of the joint-stock company, as Walter Rathenau, a businessman whose father founded the Aktiengesellschaft AEG in 1883, suggests:

> The de-individualisation of ownership simultaneously implies the objectification of the thing owned. The claims to

ownership are subdivided in such a fashion, and are so mobile, that the enterprise assumes an independent life, as if it belonged to no-one; it takes on an objective existence...[188]

By belonging to no-one, it becomes a real thing in its own right. The Bill and the Charter and the company model it follows present the Bank as an autonomous object separate from any individuals. Its incorporation, the making of something into a body, is part of its validity as an organization, and remains so. This object is then given its own name – 'The Governor and Company of the Bank of England' – which it retains, despite being popularly known simply as the Bank of England since the time of Governor Richardson (1973–83).

The credibility of an organization or of a novel is bound up with it being seen as an objective entity, of having an ontology that is separate from particular individuals. This has important later legal and political ramifications as has been highlighted by Jeroen Veldman when he suggests that the reification and singularity of the incorporated company is one of the factors that has led to its inconsistency and incoherence in legal and political terms.[189] Corporations can sometimes be treated as fictional persons with rights, sometimes as bundles of contracts, sometimes as specters that can refuse responsibility. Since a corporation is not a body, does not have intentions or desires, then what species of being can it be? What sort of thing can appear sometimes and claim immortality, and disappear at others, becoming no more than an assemblage of agreements between people? The broader question of just who then is doing the organizing, the projecting – or the writing in the case of the novel – is one that we turn to next.

The death of the projector

In the novel, Defoe has to disappear from the story if it is to be taken as an object and true to itself. In this process of disappearing he takes on several guises which progressively remove him from the text. Bear in mind that the novel, like virtually everything Defoe published, was published with no author's name, just the printer and the bookseller. In the Preface the tone is very much that of the writer, whoever they were, speaking directly to the reader, equal to equal. The writer initially presents himself as rather hard-done-by and deserving of sympathy. His text, he complains, is likely to be misunderstood because 'there are so many romances around that this, the genuine private history', will be mistaken for one of these lesser forms. But Defoe uses 'we' to concede that 'we must be content to leave the Reader to pass his own Opinion'.[190] It is not clear exactly who this 'we' is, it may be the royal or authorial 'we', or it may refer to the myriad of people involved in the publication, or it may refer to the author and the reader. Whatever meaning is taken, it shifts ownership from Defoe. As we read on, the Author is then declared to be Moll herself, a character who is writing her own story. But even after Defoe disguises himself as Moll, we are then told that the story has been refined by 'the pen', which is presumably a synecdoche for Defoe as editor. The 'pen' has had trouble 'to wrap it up so clean, as not to give room, especially for vitious Readers to turn it to his Disadvantage'. Defoe is disappearing behind all these guises, all these disguises that are attempting to make the novel 'real'.

This seems a nice illustration of Foucault's description of the death of the author from written texts which he suggests takes place in the seventeenth or eighteenth century:

> Using all the contrivances that he sets up between himself and what he writes, the writing subject cancels out the signs of his particular individuality. As a result, the mark of the writer is reduced to nothing more than the singularity of his absence; he must assume the role of the dead man in the game of writing.[191]

Paradoxically, the death of the author in the text itself occurs at the time when the idea of an author owning the text is first given legal status. During most of Defoe's lifetime, ownership of a book was collectively shared among printer, bookseller and author. It was not until 1710 that the Statute of Anne determined that copyright automatically belonged to the author of the work. This was not an immediate change, however. The title page of *Moll Flanders*, over a decade later, mentions no author.[192] Defoe had spent much of his early writing life disguising his authorship for political reasons, but by this time is now seeking to lay claim to the ownership of the commercial success of *Robinson Crusoe* and *Moll Flanders* at the same time as he is being disguised within, or negated by, the machineries that make the text possible.

We can see the same happening with William Paterson, as the author of the Bank. The absolute certainty with which Paterson is cited as the person who initiated the Bank of England is suspicious to anyone attuned to the politics of the period. Paterson is recognized as 'the projector of the Bank of England'[193] by pamphleteers at the time; renowned and amateur historians from all periods since, whether supporters or detractors; and the current Bank of England web-site. In a letter to Queen Anne on 4th April 1709, he describes himself as the person who 'first formed and propos'd the scheme for the relieving of public credit by establishing the Bank of England'.[194] It is clear enough that Paterson could not have achieved this alone, despite his attempts to gain some reward from the Monarch. He claims to be secure in his position as 'the chief and primary projector of the Bank of England'.[195] He claims to be the cause, and the institution was the result.

But for the Bank to be seen as an independent entity it had to be seen to be cut free from its author, in just the same way that *Moll Flanders* had to be cut free from Defoe. Paterson is established as the prime projector so that he can be easily jettisoned and the Bank can continue, floating beyond human agency. He is gone within the first year. The circumstances of his departure are not clear but it is recorded in the minutes of the Court of Directors that Paterson had become involved with another project, The Orphan's Fund, which could be seen as a competitor to the Bank. This was deemed inappropriate, and Paterson resigned. To a great extent though, he had already been replaced as 'projector' by the first 'Governor', John Houblon. The author cannot remain and is removed as soon as the Bank is 'realized'. For the Bank to be taken seriously, to be given credit, it has to be seen to be delivered by an objective narrator who can embody the Bank as real, and not a creature of someone's imagination. The projector cannot survive in the same capacity once the project is up and running because the conditions of the project have changed and no longer require the person who embodies the moment when something was made from nothing. The author only has so much control; the audience defines the composition too, as do formal constraints and the logic of its own development. For the project to succeed it has finally to be thrown from its author to be realized as an independent, autonomous object with a life of its own.

Throwing forth *Moll*

Separating the author from the projection and so allowing the projection to realize itself as an autonomous object involves a throwing forth. The sense of the word 'project' in both French and German suggests this throwing forth; the project is actually in the throwing, not the thrower or that which is thrown. The French root of the word is *jeter*, whilst Heidegger in *Being and Time* uses the word *Entwerf* which is translated as project or projection, but again literally means throw forth. He suggests that the project is not the procedure or plan that results but instead that which makes the plan or project possible. There is an entanglement of intention and outcome here, of possibility and actuality, even a sense that the project discovers itself. Derrida plays with a similar idea in his essay 'Some Statements and Truisms' in which he discusses the nature of new theories using the image of a jetty:

> By the word "jetty" I will refer from now on to the force of that movement which is not yet subject, project, or object, not even rejection, but in which takes place any production and any determination, which finds its possibility in the jetty - whether that production or determination be related to the subject, object, the project, or the rejection.[196]

Derrida captures the idea of something being thrown forward, propelled or projected, which is not yet itself but discovers itself in the propulsion or projection. In this process it becomes realized as a separate, independent, impersonal object, gathering solidity as it flies.

So who throws forth *Moll Flanders,* and what happens in the throwing forth? If we begin from the perspective of the creative genius so familiar since the rise of European Romanticism, then it is if course Defoe, the author. Moll is, from this angle, his creation. It is worth considering in some detail the scenario as he sits down to write because it helps to locate the idea of a flesh-and-blood person creating something. Defoe, now in his sixties, is most probably sitting in a room in his house in Church Street, Stoke Newington. It is the street in which he was born, although his original family house burnt down in the Great Fire of London. For all the discussion of Defoe as an urbanite, this is actually a suburb of London at the time.[197] He has been married to Mary Tuffley for 38 years and has six children. His eldest son, Daniel, is married and has set up as a merchant in Cornhill. His younger son, Benjamin, has been trained for the law but is trying to make a career in journalism, working for a journal which is radically opposed to the moderating politics of Court Whigs like his father.[198] Only one daughter is married, two are still at home and actively in search of husbands. Marriage and dowries, the deals to be done, are very much on their father's mind. For many years, he has earned his living (as well as spells in prison) by his pen. He is a master craftsman of words with a wide experience of what it means to write, to publish and to make money by understanding popular taste. The creation of *Moll* can thus be easily situated in Defoe's life. The novel draws on his own six months experience of Newgate Prison, of criminal street life in London, and of money and marriage. However, control of the project and the process of projection is complex. As Defoe scratches on the white page in his room in Church Street, how does the projection emerge, how is it thrown forth?

Clark attempts some explanation. The blank page, he asserts, is never blank but 'a virtual space whose focus is neither the psyche of the writer nor yet outside it. It is a space of mediation in which what I express, is echoed back transformed'. He goes on to picture the emptiness of the blank page as 'vibrant as the place of intersection of the writer's intentionality with multiple possibilities of reading. The empty page is full of a sense of potential because it is really already a crowded page'.[199] Imagine Defoe's particular page being crowded with various characters, present in his imagination so present in the room. These characters are projecting through Defoe as he writes. Defoe acts and is acted upon, projects and is projected through.

A key figure in the room may have been Mary Carleton or Steadman (1642–73), a fraudster from the middle of the seventeenth century who became known as 'The German Princess'. Moll is very likely to have been fashioned in her image, although Hero Chalmers in an article entitled 'The Person I am, or what they made me to be' suggests that the current image of Carleton may equally have been constructed by Moll, that the fact may have been shaped by the fiction.[200] Born Mary Moders, she was married several times, and once convicted of bigamy. She had an affair with a German nobleman who gave her money and presents with which she absconded before the planned marriage. She then established herself in London as the orphaned German Princess van Wolway from Cologne and sought to marry John Carleton by pretending she had a fortune. He, however, was also pretending to wealth. She was again charged with bigamy and the case came to a very public trial. She was eventually acquitted.

Mary Carleton was probably competing for representation in the character of Moll with Moll King, or Elizabeth Adkins, proprietor of one of the most infamous coffee-houses in London and well known for her 'entrepreneurial spirit'. She was transported for stealing a gold watch, and spent time in Newgate where she may also have met Defoe.[201] These figures, and perhaps many others, are in some respects present in the room fighting for representation, fighting to project themselves and become real.

The growing popular audience outlined in chapter 3 is present in the room too with its desires and needs shaping what might be written, and what might sell. Terry Eagleton is not alone in his view that 'Defoe simply wrote whatever he thought would sell, churning out works of all kinds for the rapidly growing mass market of his day'.[202] Outside and inside the room, London, teeming with life and possibilities, provides a landscape for most of the novel. Defoe's realistic account of the physical world of London and its inhabitants in the early eighteenth century is generally regarded to be one of the chief characteristics of *Moll Flanders* and to set a precedent for realism in the genre of the novel. As Moll rushes through the streets of London, they are topographically correct. The plot too is a reflection of what was going on around the author at the time. As Paula Backscheider comments –

Moll Flanders is, of course, a novel about a criminal, and crime was very much on the minds of English People in 1720. In fact, they believed they were in the midst of an unprecedented crime wave. The so-called Black Act that was passed in 1723, the year after the publication of Moll Flanders, included the most extensive increase in the number of offences classified as capital instituted in that century.[203]

The text that emerges combines these shadowy projections – of real people, a market, a city – into something that they are not but something that it is. *Moll* becomes itself, Moll becomes herself, through the recombination of all these elements.

So many projectors vie for control of the text. Moll herself, according to several commentators, takes over the novel[204] but the bookseller and the printer also project their own ideas and desires on the shape of this text, asserting their own control. The commercial arrangements of paying by the page encouraged Defoe to rush through the tale, breathlessly piling one adventure upon another to keep the pages turning, which certainly influenced the shape and rhythm of the text. There may also have been subconscious projections. Ian Watt supposes a complex relationship between Defoe and his protagonist, arguing that Moll is more a tradesman than a woman.

> Indeed her most positive qualities are the same as Crusoe's, a restless, amoral and strenuous individualism. It is, no doubt, possible to argue that these qualities might be found in a character of her sex, station, and personal vicissitudes; but it is not likely, and it is surely more reasonable to assume that all these contradictions are the consequence of a process to which first-person narration is peculiarly prone; that Defoe's identification with Moll Flanders was so complete that, despite a few feminine traits, he created a personality that was in essence his own.[205]

All of these figures and forces are at play on the blank page. It is a crowded space, and one that produces the novel as an assemblage of materials that were already to hand.

As Defoe projects these forces, the novel – this particular novel – is thrown forth to realize itself. Clark struggles to describe this sense of something becoming, coming into being.

> Above all, the work begins to be a work when a stage is reached at which the linguistic structure is something other and more pressing than the mere externalization of personal effort or expression, when it takes on a certain force of speaking for itself, an authority whose law may dictate, impersonally, the work's future unfolding.

Quoting Blanchot's *The Space of Literature* he goes on to suggest:

> That which is glorified in the work is the work, when the work ceases in some way to have been made, to refer back to someone who made it, but gathers all the essence of the work in the fact that now there is a work – a beginning and initial decision – this moment which cancels the author.[206]

This beautiful insight into the process of throwing forth helps understand something about the nature of any project, including novels and organizations, and has implications for the writer and projector which we will discuss later. As it grows, the project demands autonomy and must be true to itself, even if that means the disposal of the projector. The creator must die in order that the creation can live.

Paterson is usually seen as the creative genius behind the Bank of England. Even those who disdain him, such as Macaulay, applaud his imagination and industry.[207] His early biographer, Saxe Bannister, eulogizes on his strength of character, energy and ability. The historian W.A. Steel builds on Bannister's portrait, describing Paterson as a 'man of genius'.[208] A more recent biographer, Forrester, entitles his account *The Man Who Saw the Future*.[209] Paterson was an adventurer, sailing and trading around the new outposts of the West Indies and South America. He combined these experiences with a talent in accounting and a persuasive enthusiasm. There is no doubt that the Bank of England that came into being required his imagination and intention; but there is also no doubt that the Bank of England that came into being was not manifested solely because of his intentions. It was not *his* Bank.

The process of projection was complex, involving multiple projectors. As we have already seen it required the projecting skills of Montague and Godfrey, of Governor Houblon, and indeed the needs and desires of the widows, merchants, tradesmen and gentry who backed it. It was constrained and shaped by the demands of parliament and the King, and the antecedent experiments in banking and incorporation in England and the Netherlands as discussed earlier. From this complex of projections and projectors emerges the Bank, owned or authored by none of them, but influenced by all of them. For example, the character of the Governor matters greatly in the official histories. He must be of standing, of moral rectitude and competent, but all this is also combined with the necessarily impersonal nature of the position. It is an 'office', a role produced by the fact of the bank, or a function of the narrative of the Bank. So all these figures may endorse 'it', shape 'it', take a stake in 'it', but the Bank is produced by none of them. It is as if the Bank finds itself in the throwing forth of these projections and then is assumed to have always been there, a project awaiting projection, an office awaiting occupation. It is as if the Bank invents itself.

The economic historian Forrest Capie uncovers the same paradox in his history of the Bank. 'No one invented central banking. The Bank, however, has had a long history as a central bank, a longer one still as a bank of monopoly issue, and an even longer one as a banker to the government'.[210] The impression given is that the Bank has always been there, and that no-one can be reliably credited with its beginnings. This inevitability is illusory but part of the being of the Bank, part of how it must function. It suggests the kind of immanence referred to in the introduction to this chapter, an inevitability which suggests it was meant to be. It realizes how it was meant to be in the process of being 'thrown forth'.

There are a myriad of projectors at work in the creation of the Bank and the novel. There is a tension between the idea of the result of the projection being true, bounded and identifiable, and an understanding of the processes that create the object from this multitude of entwined antecedent causes. The tension between these positions is manifest in every project. The needs and requirements of multiple projectors interact and coalesce into an entity which is separate from or beyond the projectors, and apparently true to itself. But in both *Moll* and the Bank other forces are also called into play, forces which none of the projectors could control or predict. In other words, there appears to be a need in both for the accidental to play a role in realizing the narrative potential of the entity.

Accidental inevitability

The opening lines of Sir John Clapham's authoritative history of the Bank of England (1944) articulate a general and particular truth: 'The establishment of the Bank of England (1694) can be treated, like many other historical events both great and small, either as curiously accidental or as all but inevitable'.[211] The expression 'curiously accidental' is wonderfully paradoxical. It conjures a sense of the uncanny in the suggestion that the accidental is not quite accidental, that there is something strange or curious about the accident. Perhaps it is not an accident at all? The paradox is compounded when it is balanced with 'inevitability'; it suggests that there may be a kind of relentless logic or guiding force at work in the accidental. This sense of the uncanny nature of the accidental inevitability of both the Bank and *Moll* is important to an understanding of the process of projecting and of the 'throwing forth' of a project.

Literary-oriented studies of the Uncanny tend to refer to Freud's essay 'Das Unheimliche'. This essay begins with a discussion of the etymology of the German word *Unheimlich*. *Heimlich* means familiar, belonging to the home or known, so *Unheimlich* can therefore be seen as unfamiliar or strange, not known, not homely. However, Freud (in his typically allusive style) demonstrates that there are further complexities. *Heimlich* can also be taken to mean secret, hidden in the home, so *Heimlich* and *Unheimlich* can be seen to echo, rather than oppose, each other. They rest upon each other. Freud takes 'un' to mean in this case, not a negative but a repression. He sees the uncanny as 'something familiar and old-established in the mind that has been estranged by the process of repression'.[212] We are approaching the uncanny from this sense as signaling something unknown but recognized, a secret which is apprehended and understood, but kept a secret nonetheless. Nicholas Royle brings out the paradoxical nature of the uncanny/canny in the opening to his book of that name:

> But the uncanny is not simply an experience of strangeness or alienation. More specifically, it is a peculiar commingling of the familiar and unfamiliar. It can take the form of something familiar unexpectedly arising in a strange and unfamiliar context, or of something strange and unfamiliar unexpectedly arising in a familiar context. It can consist in a sense of homeliness uprooted, the revelation of something unhomely at the heart of hearth or home … A feeling of uncanniness may come from curious coincidences, a sudden sense that things seem to be fated or 'meant to happen'.[213]

The narratives of *Moll* and the Bank both share this quality of accidental inevitability, which gives an uncanny sense that they were meant to be, projections which were waiting to happen, waiting to be established.

Although *Moll Flanders* gives the impression of reporting a tale of what would generally be likely to happen to a character like Moll, in actual fact accident, and indeed the supernatural, intervene on several occasions to move the plot along. It is surely uncanny that a man Moll tricks into marrying her for a fortune she does not possess turns out to be her half-brother and she is thus reunited with the mother who 'pleaded her belly in Newgate' and gave Moll up. 'Let anyone judge the Anguish of my Mind', Moll vents after her husband's mother has been telling her life story, including her real name and her experiences in Newgate, 'when I came to reflect, that this was certainly no more or less than my own Mother, and I now had two Children, and was big with another by my own Brother, and lay with him still every Night'.[214] This uncanny aspect of plot development, of coincidences tragic and comic, is familiar in the novel of the early eighteenth century and, of course, in many later plots driven by a series of remarkable events.

Defoe goes further than the uncanny when he calls on the supernatural to move the plot along. When Moll first succumbs to stealing goods there is the suggestion that events are beyond her control; that she is in the grip of the devil.

> Being brought, as I may say, to the last Gasp, I think I may truly say I was Distracted and Raving, when prompted by I know not what Spirit, and as it were, doing I did not know what, or why: I dress'd me... and went out, I neither knew or considered where to go, or on what Business; but as the Devil carried me out and laid his Bait for me, so he brought me to be sure to the place, for I knew not whither I was going or what I did.[215]

It is worth remembering that Defoe, and many others of his time, did seem to think of the devil as more than just a metaphor. In his *Political History of the Devil* of 1726, Defoe is clear that there are secret forces in the world, whether as witchcraft or whispers in a suggestive ear. When her con-man husband Jemy has deserted Moll in the coach house in Chester, after he finds out that she has no money, the supernatural is again called on. He asks her whether she has a business, land, investments, even money in the Bank of England,[216] and she says nothing. It is when she pretends to honesty, telling him that she never lied (which is in itself something of a deceit), that Jemy realizes that they have defrauded each other and leaves. He apparently returns, from 'a Place about 12 miles off', because he heard her cry out 'Oh Jemy! oh Jemy! Come back, come back.'[217] Moll is astonished because she did indeed cry out. The incident establishes a strong connection between the two characters which will be played out in the novel. Not that Moll ever loses her head, because she refrains from quoting the rest of what she cried out in his absence: 'I'll give you all I have'.[218] Moll is always careful in the actual event never to give Jemy all she has, not even her real name.

Accident, the supernatural and the uncanny all play important roles in *Moll Flanders* and the novel as a genre. Indeed, Defoe drew attention to these as characteristics of projecting in general in his *Essay upon Projects*. As outlined previously, he muses over the fact that some of the most hazardous projects turn out to be successful. It would therefore be blasphemous to condemn them because providence has blessed them. In other words, their success is their justification. The example he gives of such a project is the tale of the treasure seeker and the first royally-appointed governor of the Province of Massachusetts Bay, Sir William Phips, of whom much more will be said later. Phip's tale is at the heart of our book. Not only does Defoe cite it as the example of the uncanny, the accidental, and the providential in projects, but it is also central to the emergence of the Bank of England. Without the success of this treasure-seeking adventurer, the Bank of England as we know it would not have come to be. Gold and silver discovered in the blue depths of the Caribbean propelled the story that we tell here.

The specific metaphor of an invisible hand is brought into play in *Moll* to help with plot development and to ensure that the narrative logic of the novel is realized. Having disentangled herself from the incestuous relationship with her brother and the children produced by it, Moll returns to London, but planning a trip north, looks for somewhere to keep her valuables. She wants an institution she can trust, and is recommended to try a bank. There she finds her new husband, a clerk in the bank and a sober, safe bet. 'I Liv'd with this Husband in the utmost Tranquillity', she says, 'I kept no Company, made no visits; minded my Family, and oblig'd my Husband; and this kind of Life became a Pleasure to me'. But the momentum of the narrative demands that this is not to last, for nothing ever does in Moll's life. Moll reports that she 'liv'd in an uninterrupted course of ease and Content for Five Years, when a sudden Blow from an almost invisible Hand, blasted all my Happiness and turn'd me out into the World'.[219] The Banker dies and Moll is left to fend for herself yet again.

The image of an 'almost invisible hand' is arresting. It is presumably 'almost' invisible because Moll is capable of following the train of events that led to this calamity. The Banker lent money to a clerk, who lost it. The Banker's fortunes could not sustain the loss so he 'grew Melancholy and Disconsolate, and from thence Lethargick, and died'.[220] There is a series of events here that nobody planned, but in which a pattern can be discerned, a pattern that is repeated time and again in Moll's life story. As Carl Levitt notes in his article 'Defoe's Almost Invisible Hand',[221] every time Moll is settled and secure something happens, an invisible hand intervenes and sends her out into the world again to make her own way.

The invisible hand propelling the narrative along might be Defoe's, in that he is penning the story, but he is writing as if he is Moll, so her character must also to some extent dictate what is likely to happen. To make matters more complex, he is writing for a market which shapes the structure, topics and incidents if the book is to sell. As the narrative gains pace and begins to manifest a life of its own, so is there a sense that it must fulfil its own requirements as a narrative, and hence dictate its own terms. The metaphor of an invisible hand is a way in which we might describe this complex interweaving of needs, desires and probabilities. Clark, in his study of inspiration, gives several examples of a force taking over writing, of writers who felt that they were possessed. It is recorded of Keats, for example, that:

> He has often not been aware of the beauty of some thought or expression until after he has composed and written it down. It has then struck him with astonishment – and seemed rather the production of another person than his own.[222]

Many authors provide accounts of their possession by ideas, of characters needing to do a particular thing, of writing involving 'a sense of dispossession and uncertainty of agency during composition'.[223] Forces beyond the comprehension of the author shape the text, and forces beyond the comprehension of the projector shape all projects.

If we turn to the Bank of England, then its antecedents are well rehearsed: the war with France; the promissory notes of the goldsmith bankers in London; the development of banks abroad, and so on, are all lined up to explain its development. To some extent, the story has been tidied up and rationalized, as if certain causes simply led to certain effects. But the story we uncover carries far more of the accidental and uncanny; a story much more consonant with Foucault's idea of a genealogy, which is far from a neat succession of events that led progress to the present. Instead, this is a history that seeks to 'identify the accidents, the minute deviations – or conversely, the complete reversals – the errors, the false appraisals, and the faulty calculations that gave birth to those things that continue to exist and have value for us; it is to discover that truth or being does not lie at the root of what we know and what we are, but the exteriority of accidents'.[224] The Bank of England emerges as much out of accident and an uncanny series of events as from anyone's plan or the unfolding of a particular historical inevitability.

The story of the Bank is entangled with the fortunes of a treasure hunter from New England, William Phips (1651–95). He encapsulates the idea of a projector, with extraordinary successes based on risky gambles. Born the son of a shipwright in Maine, Phips (claimed to be one of 26 children) learned the trade too. He married a shipwright's widow, presumably coming into some money, and went to sea. In 1683, 'cap-in-hand',[225] he came to England to secure financial backing for voyages to search for Spanish treasure. The projects were, as Defoe indicates in *An Essay upon Projects*, a long shot. After several fairly unsuccessful expeditions, Phips's tale caught the ear of Christopher Monck, the Duke of Albermarle, a disreputable aristocrat and pioneer of boxing who had squandered his family inheritance on horse racing and gambling, a favorite pastime of the period.[226] Monck backed the project in one last gamble to repair his fortune. Phips's plan was to use the new 'diving machines', one of Defoe's abortive investments too, to search for the Spanish galleon, the *Nuestra Señora de la Concepción*, which had sunk 50 years before off the Bahamas. But the galleon was elusive; they searched in vain and finally in January 1687 Phips gave the order that they were to head for home, empty-handed.

> On that last day, some of the divers went looking for mementoes of the trip. As they explored a relatively shallow reef close to the shore they chanced upon a spectacular plume of coral reef … they decided to take pieces of it home … But when they dived to look more closely they saw beneath it the

unmistakable shape of a large cannonball ... The Senora de la Concepcion had been found.[227]

The booty was immense: 68,511 pounds of silver and a little gold. Clapham reports that the 'company paid 10,000 per cent and divided a sum equal to a fifth of the national revenue'.[228] Paterson was one of the investors. His early biographer Saxe Bannister reports that Paterson had significantly augmented his own wealth and so established himself as a wealthy merchant in London by taking a stake in Phips's voyage 'to raise 300,000 from a sunken Spanish galleon'.[229] Paterson had taken a risk that paid off. This accident seems to have been formative to the Bank. The huge bounty from Phips' voyage acted like a beacon to other projectors, including of course those who met at the Sun Tavern and were interested in the project of the Bank. The adventure also flooded the market with bullion, the goldsmiths could not cope, and so it further emphasized the need for a bank. Phips was also knighted and later became the first significant, and probably the most charismatic, figure in Paterson's 'Society'. Finally of course, the wealth established Paterson as a significant figure and a successful projector. That is to say, his success proved that he was successful, even though he had no practical connection to the discovery of a cannonball beneath a reef near the Bahamas. Nonetheless this accident enabled the emergence of the Bank of England which is now seen as inevitable, as always having been there. There is an uncanny sense of the inevitable having been facilitated by a storm that caused a Spanish shipwreck on a coral reef on All Soul's Day in 1641, carrying treasure stolen from South America.

Oddly, economic theory shares this presentiment of the uncanny too. That an invisible force or hand guides events has become axiomatic of 'the market' since Adam Smith used the metaphor once in his 1776 *An Inquiry into the Nature and Causes of the Wealth of Nations*. It is perhaps his most famous quotation:

...every individual, therefore, endeavours as much as he can both to employ his capital in the support of domestick industry, and so to direct that industry that its produce may be of the greatest value; every individual necessarily labours to render the annual revenue of the society as great as he can. He generally, indeed, neither intends to promote the publick interest, nor knows how much he is promoting it. By preferring the support of domestick to that of foreign industry, he intends only his own security; and by directing that industry in such a manner as its produce may be of the greatest value, he intends only his own gain, and he is in this, as in many other cases, led by an invisible hand to promote an end which was no part of his intention. Nor is it always the worse for the society that it was no part of it. By pursuing his own interest he frequently promotes that of the society more effectually than when he really intends to promote it.

As Mark Thornton notes,[230] a host of academics have debated the meaning of Smith's phrase, as well as using it repeatedly to capture something about the ways in which human beings appear to be moved in patterns of which they themselves are not fully aware. The spectral hand is deemed important enough that articles are published in top-ranked economics journals and there are book-length treatments of the subject.[231] Adam Smith's use of the metaphor is generally tracked back to Shakespeare's *Macbeth*. Smith is known to have lectured on this play, and on imagery in Shakespeare in general. Having killed Duncan and ascended the Scottish throne, Macbeth must now kill Banquo in order to cover his tracks:

> Come, seeling night,
> Scarf up the tender eye of pitiful day,
> And, with thy bloody and invisible hand,
> Cancel and tear to pieces that great bond,
> which keeps me pale.[232]

Events seem to have run out of Macbeth's control; the narrative logic of his situation demands its own conclusion, another crime must be committed and a hand moves Macbeth's own.

It is notable that commentators and articles speak of *the* Invisible Hand when Smith (and, as we have seen, Defoe too) actually spoke of *an* invisible hand. The two have rather different connotations. Smith did once use the term 'the invisible hand' but this was specifically connected with early religious thought and a force of the god, Jupiter: 'Fire burns, and water refreshes; heavy bodies descend, and lighter substances fly upwards, by the necessity of their own nature; nor was the invisible hand of Jupiter ever apprehended to be employed in those matters'.[233] 'The invisible hand' would have suggested a god-like force shaping and guiding a system for the benefit of mankind. This is the meaning that has often been taken forward from Smith's treatise – as long as people pursue their own self-interest then a god-like force will look after the bigger picture. This god-like force has become known as 'the invisible hand' of the 'free market', a reified entity which decides what it likes, and what it doesn't like, and responds accordingly. 'An invisible hand' is less god-like, much more lowly and circumstantial.

The key point Smith seems to be getting at here is that the end is outside the control of the individual. Smith does not suggest that a singular invisible hand always has the benefit of mankind as its intention. He simply says that human selfish ends do not always turn out badly and indeed frequently organize society 'more effectually than when he really intends to promote it'. This is a far cry from the invisible hand of the market. Smith's supposed source, an invisible hand of the dark night that strangles pity, can hardly be seen as benevolent either, but rather a baleful and dark presence. Smith's invisible hand suggests that the course of events is not within human grasp, but that this is not a matter for huge concern because the individual often cannot realize their intentions anyway. Smith's quote suggests to us the frailty and limitations of the individual, not the theological supremacy of the market. 'An invisible hand' implies accidents and forces outside the control of the individual, fate and chance that may reward adventurers, or not.

Conclusion

The Bank and *Moll* (both person and novel) have the character of being autonomous, independent objects with the power to generate their own validity. Part of the process of establishing this autonomy is the death or removal of the author, because the author gives the game away. The presence of the author exposes the fiction, shows the deceit. No wonder that Paterson and Defoe are removed from an authorial role as a necessary part of telling the story about the autonomous object. But this removal is less of a fiction than might be presumed, because in the throwing forth of the project multiple forces, uncanny, accidental and otherwise, subject the projector to their own narrative. The projector thus becomes 'projector' as both subject and object, and the projection follows its own narrative logic to an apparently inevitable conclusion. The projector is projected by their own creation. This has ramifications for how we might tell the lives of some human beings, and these are examined in the next chapter.

5

The Projectors

So far, we have explored the remarkable similarities in the processes that gave rise to the emergence of the novel *Moll Flanders* and the Bank of England. These projects shared the same space of composition, were confronted by the same problems and used the same techniques to solve them. They are both commercial and fictional enterprises which work in similar ways, and their early revolutionary impetus should not be overshadowed by their present-day institutional respectability. The impersonal and objective nature of both, combined with a sense of their accidental inevitability, conjures the idea of invisible forces at work in how they came to be. There is a sense of the uncanny in the tale, of something inert or imaginary that comes to life, which becomes autonomous. This chapter extends the sense of the uncanny in the story of the relationship between Daniel Defoe and William Paterson. The projectors of these apparently very different institutions, which we set out to prove were conceptually and historically connected, turn out to be friends and co-projectors. They worked together. An uncanny serendipity for our tale. The story of these projector's lives is almost as rollicking a good read as *Moll Flanders.* There are political intrigues, lots of pirates, robberies, colonies, battles, triumphs and disasters, and tragedy. It is a tale we couldn't leave you without telling. Secondly, the characteristics of the projectors turn out to be characteristic of the institutions they project. Defoe, Paterson and even Moll turn out to have similar backgrounds and characteristics. These findings lead us to the unsettling question haunting this book, and its authors. Who or what is doing the projecting?

Co-projectors

Defoe and Paterson led exciting and challenging lives full of adventure, disasters, fame and ignominy. The stuff of tall tales. Their lives paralleled each other, crossing and intertwining to a remarkable extent. They have even been described as inhabiting each other's persona.[234] Defoe, born 1660, and Paterson, 1658, were both young men intended for the ministry who instead headed into trade and became merchants, both operating in London in the 1680s buying and selling goods from Holland and the Americas. Defoe was known as a hosier but is likely to have dealt in a number of goods. He was most familiar with the clothing industry but as Novak observes, 'he also handled whatever products seemed to offer an opportunity for profit'.[235]

Little can be confirmed of Paterson's early life but he is known to have travelled and traded in the West Indies and Americas. There is clear evidence of his presence in Jamaica in 1673–4[236] but in what capacity is unclear. Speculation ranges from missionary work to piracy, two occupations perhaps not so dissimilar in their adventuring as they may first appear. It is his experiences here which were to lead to his lifetime ambition to establish a trade-route through Panama, so opening up commerce between the East and the West. This ambition foundered in the fated Darien expedition, which we will explore shortly.

By the late 1680s he appears to be based in London; there is a record of him having been admitted to the livery of the Merchant Taylor's Company on 21st October 1689.[237] All sources agree that by the early 1690s he was a prosperous and recognized merchant in the City of London. Bannister reports that he lived in a well-appointed house in Queen Square, Westminster and had a handsome horse and carriage with his own emblem.[238] He established himself as a valued projector with the creation of the Hampstead Water Company, mentioned earlier. The rapidly growing population of London needed more supplies of clean water. Paterson put forward a proposal to set up a joint-stock company to supply water, from the springs on Hampstead Heath, to London. He sought to attract well-known names to the list of stakeholders in order to add credibility. One of the two big names he attracted was Sir Dalby Thomas, a successful London merchant trading in sugar in the West Indies and involved in the National Land Bank. He was also a man Paterson may have known through his own trading ventures in that region.[239] Thomas was also well-known to Defoe. *An Essay upon Projects* was dedicated to Sir Thomas as a recognized projector who could appreciate its sentiments. He was a commissioner for the glass tax and appointed Defoe as 'Accomptant' at a salary of £100 around 1694.[240]

It is clear enough that Paterson and Defoe were moving in the same circles. Just when they met is difficult to pinpoint. Defoe could have come across Paterson in Holland in 1685 when taking refuge after the failed Monmouth rebellion. There was an established Scottish community in Rotterdam and it is known that Paterson traded with Holland and sought support for his expedition to colonize parts of Panama there. Their meeting at this time is, however, supposition. Nonetheless, it can be safely asserted that they were involved in the same sort of activities with the same sort of people in London in the late 80s, early 90s, and are likely to have come across each other at that time. By 1700 they were certainly friends and co-projectors. They approached William III with a joint venture to colonize parts of South America. In his *Appeal to Honour and Justice* of 1715, Defoe traces his relationship with William III to his 1701 poem 'The True Born Englishman', which is an ironic attack on the idea of a 'pure' Englishman and on nationalism in general. It defends William III and the Dutch influence on England.

How this poem was the Occasion of my being known to His Majesty; how I was afterwards received by him; how Employ'd; and how, above my capacity of deserving,

Rewarded, is … mention'd here as I take all Occasions to do for expressing the Honour I ever preserv'd for the Immortal and Glorious memory of the Greatest and Best of Princes, and whom it was my Honour and Advantage to call master as well as Sovereign.[241]

However, P.N. Furbank and W.R. Owens, two critics well known for their efforts to rationalize the Defoe canon, have challenged the idea that Defoe ever advised King William III. They point to contradictions of timing in his accounts and suggest that Defoe knew of Paterson's advisory relations with the King and invented such a role for himself, inhabiting Paterson's persona:

Defoe evidently came to know of the privileged role Paterson had been invited to play, as unofficial adviser to the king, and, as we have shown, he had some 'schemes' by Paterson in his possession. So one wonders whether this might have given him the idea of inventing a similar role for himself.[242]

This is certainly possible, and the idea of inventing a position to occupy fits nicely with our theme here, but it seems generally accepted, as in Novak's more recent work, that Defoe was some sort of adviser to William III, the King of England, and as William II, also the King of Scotland.

William Paterson is known to have been an adviser to William at this time. The historian W.A. Steel follows Bannister in asserting that around 1700 Paterson was 'resident in Westminster, incessantly occupied with matters of public interest… the trusted correspondent and agent of the ministers of William III and his successor… kindly and respectfully heard by the King himself'.[243] Armitage, in the *Dictionary of National Biography*, confirms and extends Paterson's connections with William III:

In 1701 Paterson proposed an interventionist council of trade to control Scotland's ailing economy in his *Proposal and Reasons for Constituting a Council of Trade*. The Scottish parliament did not take up his suggestion, and in London in 1701–2 he instead urged William III to revive the Darien Colony as a pan-British venture to counterbalance the Spanish-American Empire in the face of the impending crisis over the Spanish succession; he also offered the King further plans for Anglo-Scottish union and the reform of public credit.[244]

So both were advisers to William III but, more pertinently for our purposes, put forward a joint proposal to the King to colonize parts of South America. Novak includes a reference to this scheme in his biography of Defoe:

Defoe's emphasis upon the advantage of a war with Spain (in his ironically named pamphlet 'Reasons Against a War with France' written as propaganda to support William's wishes) and upon the possibility of taking away some of Spain's colonies in the New World may have had some connection with a scheme that Defoe and William Paterson presented to King William. A manuscript of this proposal, dated 12 December 1702, was in Defoe's possession and was later deposited by Defoe's descendants in the Bodleian Library. Paterson and Defoe proposed colonising the areas of South America now equivalent to the southern parts of Chile and Argentina. Defoe was to propose such an adventure again to Robert Harley in 1711, and was eventually to write a fiction-alised version of an explorative march through this area in a *New Voyage around the World* 1724.[245]

This working relationship between Defoe and Paterson was known and recognized by others. They seem to have been easily confused with one another. Just as Furbank and Owen suggest that Defoe inhabited the persona of Paterson, Saxe Bannister also notes a merging in their identity, reporting that a pamphlet entitled 'Fair Payment is no Sponge' (1717) was suggested at the time to be written 'by the said Mr Paterson or by Daniel Defoe'.[246]

Defoe came to regard Paterson as a friend. In 1703 the satirical tract 'The Shortest Way with Dissenters' landed Defoe in serious trouble. It was written in the character of a high church zealot and urged that dissenters should be hanged or banished. The tract expressed in sardonically plain English some of the views almost certainly held but never spoken by high church men. It was too much. Defoe was accused of writing a seditious libel. William III was dead, Queen Anne had taken the throne, and, on this occasion, had also taken offence. Defoe found himself a fugitive again, and it was to William Paterson that he wrote for help:

> Jayls, pillorys and such like with which I have been threaten'd
> … have convinct me I want passive courage, and I shall never
> for the future think myself injur'd if I am call'd a coward.[247]

The letter asked for help in reaching Robert Harley who was close to the Queen and could intercede on his behalf. Paterson was connected with Harley, the First Earl of Oxford, and someone who had also supported the founding of a Land Bank in 1696. Nonetheless, Defoe was captured in Spitalfields, London, and imprisoned in Newgate 'indefinitely', or until he could give evidence of good behavior. He was released after three months, and the 'evidence of good behaviour' seems to have been an agreement to work as a secret agent for Harley.[248]

Paterson and Defoe are again working side by side in 1706–7, smoothing the way for the union of England and Scotland, at that time separate countries, but sharing the same monarch. Defoe was engaged as propagandist in Scotland and was a member of the same committee as Paterson, working out the economics of the union. Novak is amused 'that among the Scottish gentry and nobility, he must have passed for an economist of genius', happy 'in the midst of things, debating the amount for the drawing back on oatmeal exported to Norway and on salt, regulating the tax on ale, and debating prices with his old friend, Sir William Paterson'.[249] Defoe and Paterson seem to have been tightly tied to Harley, and the project of the Union was a success for all of them, although Paterson seems to have been recompensed much more for his efforts than Defoe.[250] The by-now-failed Darien Company was wound up under the terms of the Union in 1707 and reparations were paid to investors.[251] Despite the huge investment, the expedition had been an unqualified disaster. The first expedition in 1698 had resulted in the loss of four of the five ships and the deaths of three quarters of the adventurers from disease and starvation. One ship and three hundred people returned in disgrace a year later. The second expedition in 1699 was no more successful, resulting in more deaths and a skirmish with the Spanish who also had a colony nearby. The project failed, but its consequence was to force the Scots to accept the Act of Union because of the bankruptcy of the country, and so a new project was born.

Paterson died in 1719. Defoe published *Robinson Crusoe* in the same year. *Moll Flanders* was to follow three years later. In this regard, we might wonder how much knowledge Defoe had of the Darien expedition. In preparation for putting forward proposals to William and his ministers, it may be supposed that they had many conversations about the South Americas, including Paterson's personal experience on that continent, the Indies, and Darien in Panama. Defoe's relationship with Paterson is likely to have influenced the material addressed and contained in several of his later novels, most notably *Robinson Crusoe* and *New Voyage around the World* (1724), a novel which, as J. McVeagh observes, 'sums up a lifetime's thought on the subject of the South Seas'.[252]

The full title of another novel he published in the same year as *Moll Flanders* expresses Defoe's enduring fascinations with travel, money and crime rather neatly – *The History and Remarkable Life of the truly Honourable Col. Jacque, commonly call'd Col. Jack, who was Born a Gentleman, put 'Prentice to a Pick–Pocket, was Six and Twenty Years a Thief, and then Kidnapp'd to Virginia, Came back a Merchant; was Five times married to Four Whores; went into the Wars, behav'd bravely, got Preferment, was made Colonel of a Regiment, came over, and fled with the Chevalier, is still abroad compleating a Life of Wonders, and resolves to dye a General.*

These were two men who dreamed of travel and adventure, sentiments which echo in the 'Scots Poem' published by Defoe in 1707:

I'd gladly breath my Air on Foreign Shores:
Trade with rude Indian, and sun-burnt Mores.
I'd speak Chines, I'd prattle African.
And briskly cross, the first meridian.
I'd pass the line, and turn the Caps about.
I'd rove, and sail the earth's great Circle out.
I'd fearless, venture to the Darien Coast;
Strive to retrieve, the former Bliss we lost,
Yea, I would view Terra Incognita.
And climb the Mountains of America.

Novak comments with fascination on these lines as precursors of the romances that would involve protagonists sailing around the world and trekking across Africa.[253] Paterson's travels are part of the imaginative weave that makes up Defoe's fiction, which underscores the idea that the novel and the Bank were generated in the same space of composition. Their 'composers' were connected, and possessed of ideas about ventures and adventuring that are very similar indeed. The projects of the novel and the Bank echo each other in the manner of the lives of their projectors. Further, the similarity in background suggests that these projectors could be seen as being projected as much as projecting, figures made by a projecting age.

The character of projectors

There are key characteristics of these two projectors that are remarkably similar and are reflected or inherited by their projects. Both of these men were dissenters, outsiders, chancers, tellers of tales and managers of uncertainty. Their stories once again echo each other.

There is a great deal of information, opinion and rumour available on the life of Defoe. People like to write about him, which seems to further contribute to his mystery. As one of his biographers, Paula R. Backscheider, observes, 'few men seem to be better subjects for a biography than Daniel Defoe'.[254] He lived in turbulent times and contributed to them on almost every front. Politically, he witnessed the restoration of the monarchy after the English Civil War and took part in the Duke of Monmouth's 1685 unsuccessful rebellion against James, escaping miraculously with his head. He acted as propagandist and secret agent for the Government of William III.[255] Economically, Defoe played his part as a merchant and tradesman, a serial entrepreneur and investor, and his 1726 book *The Complete English Tradesman* could even be regarded as the first business textbook. Finally, he is widely regarded as the founder of the English Novel, as we have already discussed. Defoe is something of a colossus standing at the head of the modern period, a renaissance man after the fact.

He was born Daniel Foe some time in 1660, probably in the London parish of St. Giles, Cripplegate. His father, James, was a butcher or tallow chandler according to the parish register, but describes himself as a merchant. The family were descended from small-scale yeoman farmers from the area just north of Peterborough. They were dissenters, believers who could not accept the authority of the Church of England and were often seen as dangerous freethinkers. The Church had tried, through various Acts of Parliament, to force dissenters to conform to its rules and practices. The Act of Uniformity (1662), for example, insisted on complete allegiance to the Church of England's prayer book. 'The newly revised Book of Common Prayer ... was according to the Act to be used exclusively in church services, with every clergyman instructed to "openly and publicly before the congregation ... declare his unfeigned assent and consent" to everything in the book'.[256] Religious meetings of more than five people were banned. The dissenters had to meet secretly in order to worship. As James Sutherland observes, these acts restricting heterodoxy meant that dissenters were 'a desperate people, harassed by severe laws, and at the mercy of bullies and informers and of all who happened to bear them a personal grudge'.[257]

The influence of this experience on the life of Defoe and on the novel has been fully explored in a number of biographies. Most biographers attribute great significance to the role of covert dissent in shaping Defoe's personality, his life experiences and perhaps even the shape of the Early English novel itself. Richetti concludes that 'Defoe's life from his earliest years is profoundly involved in the complex fate of being an English dissenter during these turbulent times. An angry marginality and a lingering resentment of the ruling elite, as well as of isolated auto-didacticism, such as one finds expressed in much of his writing, might well be traced to his growing up among this embattled minority'.[258] Maximillian Novak surmises that Defoe's 'sense of his own rightness on issues of conscience, and his unwillingness to accept the possibility that he might have acted improperly, may have proceeded from a profound conviction that since he was among those elected for eternal salvation, he could never be wrong in any matter of importance'.[259]

Paterson was also a dissenter, though information on him is by contrast scant, and biographies few and partisan. He was born into 'agricultural obscurity'[260] in April 1658, in Skipmyre, Dumfrieshire, Scotland; the son of John and Elizabeth Paterson, small-scale farmers. This area of Scotland was strongly Presbyterian and there is evidence to suggest that Paterson's family were Covenanters, a particular species of religious dissenter. After the Restoration of the monarchy, Charles II tried to place Bishops back into to the Church of Scotland. This was unacceptable to most Protestants who held that all men are equal before God, and hence that such earthly hierarchies had no justi-fication. Those who resisted the King's demands became known as 'Covenanters' – supporters of the Covenant, a petition drawn up in Edinburgh, originally to oppose Charles I. Forrester notes that 'the greatest concentration of these new Covenanters lay in South-west Scotland, the district where Paterson's family lived. On Sundays many of them held secret church services in the hills rather than cross the door of a church run by government-appointed Bishops. They risked fines and imprisonment'.[261] It cannot be proved that Paterson's family were active Covenanters but there is evidence that William's father refused to swear the prescribed oath of loyalty to the Bishops.[262]

This dissenting experience shaped the lives and opportunities of Defoe and Paterson in similar ways, and again informs the nature of the novel and the organization. As a persecuted and disenfranchised minority, excluded to a large extent from public life, dissenters tended to work in commerce in the new emerging financial order that was to transform Britain. 'They achieve', notes the historian David Ogg, 'success and power disproportionate to their numbers'.[263] Dissenting fostered and reflected the idea that established authorities, be they church or state, spiritual or temporal, could be challenged. However, the particular brands of dissent practiced by Defoe and Paterson gave them both an experience of acting in secret, of being outsiders to the estab-lishment because of what they believed to be true. It might have cultivated a sense in which lies are necessary to protect truth, and

sinuous forms of deceit form the warp and weft of the experienced world. Although there are psychological aspects that can
be extrapolated from this experience for Defoe, as suggested
above, and no doubt similarly for Paterson, it also shaped their
lives in very practical ways. It made them outsiders, and this
status is inherited and inherent in the novel and the organization.

Dissenters were excluded from public office and from
attending university by various Acts of Parliament passed
between 1662 and 1675. This led to a number of academies being
established to educate them, and their freedom from the
constraints of a classical education opened up new possibilities
of learning. As Novak comments: 'Unlike Universities, the
academies were open to new ideas ... For example, Locke's
Treatise Concerning Human Understanding, which was attacked by
traditional authorities, became a standard text for discussion in
the Academies.'[264] The traditional curriculum in universities
tended to concentrate on Greek and Latin texts, while the
dissenting academies studied Geography, History and Politics.
Plain English, the vernacular, rather than Classical Rhetoric, was
promoted. Defoe attended one of the very best academies, one
led by Charles Morton in Newington Green (in those days a
village north of London). Morton later became Vice-president of
Harvard College, and expounded the basic Humean empiricist
belief 'that there was nothing in the mind but what sense
perception brought into it'.[265] He directed attention to the
physical world and to the new ideas of those, like Isaac Newton,
who were exploring the world that experiments revealed.
Indeed, Newton's interests were multiple too, in finance and
science. Despite coming from a yeoman family background, he
was appointed Master of the Mint in 1699, and practiced alchemy
and magic alongside his respectable sciences of optics and
mechanics. No form of knowledge was alien to him – science or
superstition – even if he refrained from publishing much of his
alchemical and biblical work. As he was supposed to have said:

'we build too many walls and not enough bridges'.

Despite, or perhaps because of, his modern education Defoe is regarded as an outsider by significant social and professional groups of the period. He was an outsider to the circle of literary men of letters such as Alexander Pope, Jonathan Swift and Joseph Addison, as we discussed earlier. Novak observes, 'When Swift mocked Defoe's ignorance, he invited the derision of those belonging to a relatively select club (the men of letters) toward those outside the group'.[266] No wonder Defoe responds with such skepticism concerning the narrow manners of scholars and gentlemen, and repeatedly argues that ordinary people are perfectly capable of noble behavior too.

Very little is known of Paterson's education. His first serious biographer, Saxe Bannister (1790–1877) states that 'The story of his early days is still obscure, although traditional accounts are not wanting of his intellectual culture, and of his earnest religious disposition, in youth. The abandonment of his career in the ministry of the Church of Scotland, in consequence of persecutions, was soon followed by his voluntary exile; and by the change of his destination from that of ministry to trade.'[267] The historian W.A. Steel in an article published in *The English Historical Review* in 1896 suggests that 'his education was limited to what could be obtained in a Scotch parish school', but insists that more than one passage of his writings affords evidence that he certainly had the intellectual capacities proper to an 'enlightened merchant'. He quotes a passage from 1703 when Paterson was trying to form a public library of trade finance:

> Trade and revenues never yet have been truly methodised or digested – nay, nor perhaps but tolerably considered by any. Trade and revenues are here put together, since the public (or indeed any other) revenues are only parts or branches of the income or increase by and from the industry of the people.[268]

Quite apart from his interest in the practical matters of trade, Paterson's writing does not suggest a classical education. He, like Defoe, favors clarity and plain English, and not the decorated allusions to myth common to scholars.

Paterson is also recognized to be an outsider. He is an outsider not only by his dissenting religion but by virtue of being a Scot. Mocking, disparaging references appear frequently in regard to his Scottish descent. The historian, Thomas Babington Macaulay (1800–1859), points this up by suggesting that Paterson's co-directors at the Bank, who were

> citizens of ample fortune and of long experience in the practical part of trade, aldermen, wardens of companies, heads of firms well-known in every Burse throughout the civilised world, were not well pleased to see among them in Grocer's Hall a foreign adventurer whose whole capital consisted in an inventive brain and a persuasive tongue. Some of them were probably mean enough to dislike him for being a scot.[269]

Sir John Clapham slips into the same class-inflected disdain, referring to Paterson as 'a wanderer, probably like many other Scots, a peddler turned merchant. He had become a merchant tailor by redemption – paying for it.'[270] In other words, he bought his status with money, and was not born into it.

Defoe and Paterson are both frequently presented as victims of their status, even jointly so. Thomas Bateson suggests that Defoe 'like his friend Paterson was never more than a hanger-on of the ministry, an occasional agent of small account. Always pushed aside by luckier men, always poorly paid, whether from Harley's private purse or from the exchequer, he could often only compel recompense for dangerous toil by long and bitter complaint.'[271] There was no entitlement for either of these two, no silver spoon or easy social connections. In a letter addressed to the Queen in 1709 Paterson also presents himself as someone who deserves more than he has been given:

To the Queen's Most Excellent Majesty
The Humble Petition of William Paterson,
Sheweth–
That your Petitioner first formed and proposed the scheme for the relieving the public credit by establishing the Bank of England; but that not withstanding the signal success of that institution for the public service, and his unwearied endeavours in promoting the same through all manner of opposition, from 1691 to the full establishment thereof in 1694, your petitioner never had any recompense for his great pains and expence therein.[272]

There is a sense here in which power always needs to be flattered, but such a tone suggests that Paterson felt that his talents were not recognized, and hence also not properly rewarded. Given that he had probably lost a considerable amount of money on the Darien adventure, such pleading might have been economically necessary too.

Outsiders who are successful tend to be treated as upstarts. But perhaps really new ideas generally require upstarts. Defoe and Paterson take their fair share of flak from significant numbers of commentators, much of it is simply offensive. They were seen as arrogant, confident, opinionated individuals who did not like to toe the line. Paterson is scorned as having 'a reputation for double-dealing and insincerity, as well-earned as that for imagination and persuasiveness'. Perhaps as a consequence 'he soon overreached himself'.[273] Defoe is similarly mocked as being 'so grave, sententious, dogmatical a rogue that there is no enduring him', as well as being 'a garrulous know-it-all'.[274] Another commentator dismisses Paterson in the following way, in terms that could easily apply to Defoe too:

[He] seems to have been one of those men whose ideas range some years ahead of their time and who have a streak of the true visionary about them, but in whom intellect outruns intelligence and whose ingenuity may sometimes approach, but never quite reaches, genius.[275]

There is a tone to the comments above which implies that Defoe and Paterson have got above themselves in some way. This tone is still played out. At a recent conference on the Glorious Revolution, one of us asked the historian Steven Pincus for his view of Paterson. 'A bit of a chancer', was the verdict given with a wry smile. Defoe was dismissed by many commentators of the eighteenth century as a good liar and a hack writer, very much someone who chanced his arm in the hope of success, of a coincidence of public good and private benefit. Of course, had they not both been chancers, opportunists with a brass neck, there would be no story to tell.

Whether the novel and the Bank are both still regarded as chancers for the established authorities of our time is a moot point. Some commentators suggest that the novel is an outsider to the literary tradition, still 'an upstart' as suggested by Marthe Robert earlier and Terry Eagleton's well-known description of the English novel as 'a mongrel among literary thoroughbreds'.[276] Claudio Guillan suggests pretty much the same:

The modern novel, of course, from Cervantes to our time, could be described as an "outsider" model that writers insist on regarding as essentially incompatible with the passage from an unwritten poetics to an "official" system of genres.[277]

In an era of literary festivals and prizes, of Creative Writing courses and agents with smart London offices, the novel might be seen as less challenging now than it was. The Bank, despite its recognized status as an agency of the State, remains politically positioned outside the established powers of Parliament and the Treasury, who each still seek to influence the Old Lady. To some extent, in Britain, any commercial organization inherits this outsider status. It can never be considered aristocratic or noble because it lives by the profit motive and is hence always tainted by the vulgarity of money. It might build grand headquarters, but that does not guarantee respect from old money, from those who have been to the right schools as opposed to the shiny Business Schools. For the English elites, a commercial organization is, in the end, just a temporary arrangement for selling some baubles and as any brief scan of business history reveals, they come and go. Perhaps these organizations bear the same relationship to 'the establishment' as the novel bears to 'literature' – still tainted by the smell of new money.

Ventures and adventures

Defoe and Paterson were adventurers, restless characters who sought out high-risk situations. Defoe enjoyed being at the center of the action. In 1685, when he has only been married for a year and is just beginning to establish a successful business as a hosier and merchant, trading miscellaneous goods to Europe and America, he joins a rebellion led by the Duke of Monmouth, an illegitimate son of the Anglican Protestant Charles II, against the newly crowned Catholic James II. It is a disaster. In July Monmouth's forces are defeated and scattered at the battle of Sedgemoor in Somerset. Many are taken prisoner and are hanged, drawn and quartered, and then their bodies are posted by the roadside to warn others of their fate. Luckier captives are shipped out to the colonies. Those who escaped seem to have fled into the West Country, across to Protestant Holland or even to New England, where William Phips was later to become Governor. There is speculation that Defoe sought refuge in Holland and came into contact with the Scottish community there, including Paterson.[278] Richetti treats this episode as an example of Defoe's 'rashness', whilst Novak gently mocks, picturing Defoe riding forth in the 'manner of Don Quixote'.[279] Backscheider is more sympathetic, pointing out that few of the rebel soldiers were from London, but several were Defoe's friends from Morton's dissenting Academy, three of whom died.[280] Defoe miraculously escaped and in 1687 was allowed to purchase a pardon for around £60.[281] After the Glorious Revolution in 1688, he became an ardent supporter of William III and he continued to support the Protestant and, in particular, the dissenting cause throughout his life.

Nonetheless, Defoe's business interests suffered during his exile, and perhaps never completely recovered. Defoe invested in several projects after his pardon, underwriting marine insurance, importing wine from Portugal, and most famously purchasing a diving bell to search for treasure and a civet cat farm for making perfume. All eventually failed and he lost a good deal of money. In October 1692 he was declared bankrupt and imprisoned. Defoe's business projects are often mocked but Rebecca Connor notes that however odd his business schemes may have been, they had made Defoe money. By 1692, he was known as a fairly well-off merchant – 'certainly he prided himself on appearing so. He was known to wear huge wigs, extravagant clothes and most notably, a large and raffish diamond ring on his little finger.'[282] When he was declared bankrupt, his debts totaled around two million pounds in today's terms.[283] He lost his home and his business, and his wife and children were forced to live upon the charity of friends and family. Released some time in 1693, he rejoined his family and continued the hosiery business. However, his debts were not discharged, which meant that he had to hide from creditors.

Whatever we might make of Defoe's impulsiveness, Novak concedes that he does seem to have encountered some 'bad fortune' in business ventures. In June 1693 a fleet of 400 ships, 'heavily laden',[284] was attacked and taken by a French force, just as almost all Moll's possessions were stolen by 'a Pyrate' on her first trip to America. Defoe was amongst those who had insured the ships. In his 1715 autobiographical *Appeal to Honour and Justice*, one of the few pieces of writing published under his own name during his lifetime, Defoe recounts some of his business dealings in the mid-1690s.

Misfortunes in Business having unhing'd me from Matters of Trade, it was about the year 1694, when I was invited by some Merchants, with whom I had corresponded abroad, and some also at home, to settle at Cadiz in Spain, and that with offers of very good Commissions; but Providence, which had other Work for me to do, plac'd a secret Aversion in my Mind to quitting England upon any account, and made me refuse the best Offers of that kind, to be concern'd with some eminent Persons at home, in proposing Ways and Means to the Government for raising Money to supply the Occasions of the War then newly begun. Some time after this, I was, without the least Application of mine, and being then seventy miles from London, sent for to be Accomptant to the Commissioners of the Glass Duty, in which Service I continued to the Determination of their Commission.[285]

Paterson also seems to have courted adventure. He travelled widely in both Europe and the Americas. He appears to have had a home in the Bahamas where he was married to Elisabeth Turner, the widow of Thomas Bridge, a minister of the gospel in New England. Forrester suggests that Paterson would have acquired a reasonable dowry and 'nest-egg' from the marriage. Elisabeth died in the Bahamas. His enemies told stories of Paterson 'buccaneering' round the South Seas, a pirate, whilst others described him as a successful merchant trader or as a missionary.[286] On his return to London he 'took up residence in a terraced house in Denmark Street, a stone's throw from the parish church of St. Giles in the Field'.[287] By the early 1690s he was a wealthy and respected merchant. Some of this wealth had come from his investment in the high-risk project of Sir William Phips, the projector of uncanny good fortune depicted by Defoe in the *Essay upon Projects*.

Paterson also suffered his own disasters. The Bank of England was a risky venture, as explored earlier, but a huge success. The biggest and most enterprising project of Paterson's life, however, was the Darien expedition. Throughout his life he sought to establish some kind of colony around the area now called Panama to facilitate trade between the East and West, so challenging Spanish domination of trade in South America and the Indies. In this he failed. The ill-fated 'Darien enterprise', as it became known, led by Paterson in 1698, tried to establish a colony under the Scottish flag. England did not support the venture. William III was too engrossed in the war with France and seems to have thought that this venture could lead him into war with Spain too. English merchants would not support it either. If Scotland had succeeded in the venture, it could have threatened England, strangling her trade routes. Macaulay reports that one peer in the House shouted, 'If these Scots have their way, I shall go settle in Scotland, and not stay here to be made a beggar'.[288] Partly because of these sort of fears, this was a solely Scottish funded venture. Every Scotsman who could raise enough money bought a subscription.[289] The total figure amounted to about a quarter of the money in circulation in Scotland. A lot of people were prepared to take a gamble on Paterson.

On 1st November 1698 Paterson and the Scottish fleet anchored close to the Isthmus of Darien:

> They were pleased with the aspect of a small peninsular about three miles in length and a quarter of a mile in breadth, and determined to fix here the city of New Edinburgh, destined, as they hoped, to be the great emporium of both Indies.[290]

Spain was outraged. France, also with dependencies in the West Indies, was equally outraged and offered support to Spain. England was outraged and prohibited any communication with this 'nest of buccaneers'.[291] The Scots rejoiced. Their project had been established. The news from New Caledonia was good. 'The colonists, it was asserted, had found rich gold mines ... the rainy season had not proved unhealthy ... the aboriginal tribes were friendly ... The riches of the country ... were great beyond imagination.'[292] Several more ships set out from Scotland to join the adventure. They found utter ruin. The weather, the terrain and disease, had defeated the colonists. The mortality rate rose to ten or twelve a day. Both the clergymen who had accompanied the expedition died. Paterson's second wife and child died of the fever. Paterson himself succumbed to illness. The colonists decided to flee back to New England because they could not repel an expected attack by the Spanish. Paterson begged to be left behind with a small number of men but they carried him on board the *Saint Andrew*. Macaulay reports that 'Of two hundred and fifty persons who were on board the *Saint Andrew*, one hundred and fifty fed the sharks of the Atlantic before Sandy Hook was in sight. *The Unicorn* lost all its officers, and about one hundred and forty men, *The Caledonia* ... threw overboard a hundred corpses'. According to sources, Paterson lost his mind for a time. He certainly succumbed to a delirium brought on by fever.[293] Macaulay tells us he had been 'completely prostrated by bodily and mental suffering. He looked like a skeleton. His heart was broken. His inventive facylties and his plausible eloquence were no more; and he seemed to have sunk into a second childhood.'[294] The venture virtually bankrupted Scotland and effectively forced the Union of England and Scotland in 1707. One project had failed, and had become a precondition for a different sort of project. After his recovery, Paterson was one of the chief negotiators of the Union.

Defoe and Paterson were at the center of high-risk events in the late seventeenth and early eighteenth century. They were both extremely successful in some ventures and failed dismally in others. Many pay testament to their indefatigable energy and industry.[295] Defoe produced 15,000 pages of print in the year that *Moll* was published alone, a 'miraculously productive year'.[296] Both are seen or see themselves as heroic individuals. Defoe rides off in the manner of Quixote to Monmouth's rebellion, or stands up in Parliament in defense of groups such as the Kentish weavers.[297] Paterson presents himself as the heroic savior of the Scots economy, someone who would bring El Dorado to Caledonia. *Moll Flanders* and the Bank reflect these qualities of their authors; they are high-risk institutions. Part of their reason for being is to try and exploit risk and uncertainty. This is an essential characteristic of the novel and the organization; it is part of how they 'work'. Each manages anxiety with a promise that all will be well, that we are in good hands. In the novel we are in the hands of the kindly narrator, the 'pen', as we have heard. In the Bank we are in the hands of the competent Governor, and our interests are in safe hands. But such promises are lies, because any project requires arrogance and chutzpah. Both supply readers and investors with a visible structure that holds the risk, but the risk is still there, nonetheless. These are narratives that we can believe in, tales well-told.

That Defoe was a profligate teller of tales is self-evident, but some critics have related the emergence of the novel itself to Defoe's blurring of fact and fiction in his life. They suggest that the novel plays with this blurring, in the realism of its duplicity it echoes the endless simulations that the humbly born Daniel Foe traded in. Lennard Davis makes this connection explicit in his book *Factual Fictions*:

> The oddity of his own life, so filled with disguise, lies, indirection, forgery, deceit, and duplicity seems to place him constitutionally at the centre of questions about the truthfulness

of narratives, about the problem of framing and ambivalence, about the breakdown of signification and reliability.[298]

It is as if Defoe's life was a novel too, or the novel was a way of capturing a life. A life which a contemporary pamphleteer suggested was that of an '*Animal* who shifts his Shape oftner than *Proteus*, and goes backward and forward like a hunted *Hare*; a thorough-pac'd, true-bred *Hypocrite*; an *High-Church Man* one day, and a *Rank Whig* the next'.[299]

Paterson was also a teller of tales. Several commentators attest to his power to capture an audience with his imagination and eloquence. Steele for example praises his 'strong reason, and great experience', describing him as 'acquainted with commerce in all its parts, and having a natural and unaffected eloquence'.[300] Macaulay tells us that 'men spoke to him with more profound respect than to the Lord High Commissioner. His antechamber was crowded with solicitors desirous to catch some golden drops of that golden shower of which he was supposed to be dispenser'.[301] As we have noted, Paterson's writing was sometimes confused with Defoe's, and he was a recognized pamphleteer too. Finally, it is clear that the story Paterson told of the possibilities of a Scottish Eldorado captured the imagination of a nation.

Both men supported their tales with vivid and detailed accounts of goods and services, promises of money in and money out. Macaulay profiles Paterson in the following manner, but it could equally have been said of Defoe: 'He seems to have been gifted by nature with a fertile invention, an ardent temperament and great powers of persuasion and to have acquired somewhere in the course of his vagrant life a perfect knowledge of accounts'.[302] An account is also a story of course, a persuasive collection of characters and motives which is then credited as truth. Both Paterson and Defoe seem to have been interested in various types of exchanges that could then be made to circulate and so enable new possibilities. Paterson's over-riding interest in life was the circulation of trade and money, as he states clearly in his 'Brief Account of the Intended Bank of England'. The novel also circulated accounts engendering and reflecting new possibilities, new mobilities for money and people. Moll, after all, changes her station from servant girl to Gentlewoman, and finally to literary figure. She too deserves to be included in the comparison of chancers and storytellers.

Moll, Defoe and Paterson

Moll bears the same characteristics of background and character with Defoe and Paterson. She is an outsider, a high-energy, optimistic risk-taker, and a teller of tales. Like so many of Defoe's protagonists, Moll is the quintessential outsider; born in Newgate and effectively orphaned, she is outside society. Moll has to create herself from scratch. Having been placed by the authorities with a 'good motherly nurse' with the intention that she should go into service, Moll resolves against this fate preferring to become a 'Gentlewoman'. By this she means, contrary to the usage of the time, a woman who earns her own money, not someone of high birth. As we noted earlier, this resolve is mocked by the nurse who considers it a ridiculous idea, beyond the station of such as Moll.[303] Whatever Moll resorts to – trickery, theft, deceit – she never goes into service, and she always earns her own way, a statement many Gentlewomen could not make.

Moll is always outside the family, even her own family, as she disposes of children to various nurses and, when she finds her own mother, discovers that she has married her mother's son and so must once again be cast out. Moll is not only outside any kind of establishment groups but she is even outside the community of thieves, nothing being more odious to her 'than the Company in Newgate prison'.[304] She imagines herself as a unique individual, someone who prides herself on her 'invention'[305] and dexterity in tricky situations. She weaves a tale for possible suitors that they may wish to hear and one which increases her value in the marketplace of marriage between men and women. She tells her own tale, generates her own credit, insisting on her independence and ability to create herself.

Defoe and Paterson's lives parallel each other and intertwine as do *Moll Flanders* and the Bank. They are all outsiders, they are rebellious upstarts and risk-takers, full of energy and possibility, including the possibility of disaster and ruin. They all tell a tale and give an account, managing the anxiety and uncertainty of the punter who might invest. Standard descriptions of the novel echo this story. The novel does all this successfully and then becomes part of the apparatus of the literary establishment, though perhaps still not as highbrow as poetry and drama. The Bank attempts the same feat, and succeeds in emplacing itself within walls of rusticated stone. But this story reminds us that any institution is always initially an outsider, chancing risk and subject to the ridicule of those who have something to lose. All beginnings involve a challenge to others and later a claim to timelessness, to inevitability rather than accident. Not that any organization is timeless of course, as is revealed by the ceaseless history of large institutions crumbling, merging and shape-shifting.

Figuring the projector

So why do we care about this similarity, this weft of parallels and reflections? A narrative of the heroic projector seems to drive sections of this book – a narrative which can be tracked back, at least, to Defoe, Paterson and Moll Flanders in a circle of confirming self-referentiality, an argument by addition which claims that novels and organizations are mechanisms that work in the same ways. But this book is a projection too. We must not assume that others build castles in the air, while we explain evident and evidenced truths. In the case of our project, we have a sense of something that is again both necessary and accidental, meant-to-be and remarkable, as if we were being projected through, or ghost-written by an invisible hand. So who is writing here? Who or what drives the narrative? We have an uncanny feeling that Defoe has been moving our pen, that we have been propelled by him. He is the place where this projection starts and where it will end, for now.

Indeed Defoe's invisible hand seems to have shaped the modern project itself.[306] His hand can be found just about everywhere. Lennard Davis notes the range of his influence in the early eighteenth century:

> When one considers the total number of newspapers appearing in London at this time, Defoe seems to have controlled the total flow of political information to no small extent ... Defoe had under his influence *Mist's Weekly Journal, Dormer's Newsletter,* and *Mercurius Politicus* – all of which were billed as Tory newspapers, and all of which were controlled by the Whigs through Defoe's manipulation – I am not including in this list *The Flying Post.*[307]

Defoe seems to have contributed significantly to many different areas and to be considered an originator by modern commentators from all these spheres. He is the authority on a myriad of topics and disciplines. Pincus, who gives few accolades, tells us that 'Defoe, it turns out, was a remarkably perceptive historian'.[308] This commendation is echoed in the writing of economist Joel Mokyr: 'Daniel Defoe, widely regarded as the best-informed writer on the state of pre-Industrial Revolution Britain, wrote with pride on the wealth of his country, even if concerned about its future'.[309] His writing is said to have been formative on the shape and nature of journalism.[310] His three-volume *Tour Through the Whole Island of Great Britain* (1724–7) remains, according to J.H. Andrews, 'a great pioneer work of economic geography'.[311] He was involved in creating the Union between England and Scotland, which staggers on to this day.

Defoe is a founding father of modern politics, journalism, literature, economics, history and, we are claiming here, some ideas about enterprise and organization too.

The modern term for projector is entrepreneur. The two terms are synonymous, though the former had far more negative connotations. Mark Casson tracks the term entrepreneur to the early eighteenth century in the writings of the physiocratic economist Richard Cantillon (a notable projector himself) and later Jean-Baptiste Say. Both wrote in French and the term was 'variously translated into English as merchant, adventurer and employer, though the precise meaning is the undertaker of a project'.[312] The projector/entrepreneur presented by Defoe is an outsider, dissenter, account-giver and risk-taker. This is someone who is energetic, imaginative, articulate, persuasive, enthusiastic and determined – a visionary upstart or genius. This vision has the whiff of the romantic about it, if we can be allowed to read the eighteenth century through the lens of the nineteenth. The heroic Lord Byron strides across this stage, defining what it means to be a creative person with a passionate intensity. But as Byron himself would have understood, the hero has a dark side, being mad, bad and dangerous to know. The heroic narrative of the projector/entrepreneur is naive and one-sided. If we only understand it in this way we do a great disservice to the complexity of Defoe's portrayal of projectors and the analyses of the novel and the organization that we have offered here.

Projectors can be understood as twinkly-eyed outsiders with energy and optimism and sheer chutzpah, but also as conniving, deceitful, arrogant and careless rogues. Indeed, these latter qualities are necessary, not incidental, to the project. The projector is a deeply ambivalent figure, as is so illuminatingly pre-figured in Defoe's *Essay upon Projects* where 'contemptible projectors' and 'honest projectors' are really only distinguished from one another by the success of their projects. As Yamamoto suggests, 'the project was at best a vision of a future society and an audacious plan about realizing that vision through collective action'. But, at worst, it was fraud put forward by a 'rent-seeker who pretended public service to pursue their self-interest ... at the expense of people's rights and properties'.[313]

Defoe's protagonists have their dark sides. There is a structure to *Moll* which suggests that Defoe was pushing the limits of what the reader could accept from the hero, and from the author. The narrative follows a distinct pattern of declaring one thing to be so absolutely bad or evil it could never happen; and then it happens. The whole plot exhibits this pattern. The Preface defensively declares that the story will demonstrate the moral that evil will be punished and good rewarded. Yet this is patently not the case because Moll builds her final happiness on the proceeds of a life of crime. This pattern is repeated at every stage. When the older brother, who has been Moll's lover, tries to persuade her to accept his younger brother's proposal, Moll declares: 'I could never be persuaded to love one brother and Marry another',[314] and then promptly marries the younger brother. Later in the tale, having had a child to her lover Jemy, she needs to dispose of the child if she is to be able to find another husband. She explains in detail why a mother giving up the care of her child is such a reprehensible action.

> Since this Care is needful to the Life of Children, to neglect them is to Murther them; again to give them up to be manag'd by these People, who have none of that needful Affection, plac'd by Nature in them in the highest Degree, nay, in some it goes further, and is a Neglect in order of their being Lost; so that 'tis even an intentional Murther, whether the Child lives or dies.[315]

She then gives her child up to care so she can leave unencumbered. It is as if Defoe is playing with his readers, trying to see how bad he can make Moll and yet retain the reader's interest and sympathy. It is interesting in this respect that the catalogue of crimes includes that most taboo of acts, incest, although this seems to have been a popular topic in the period. But it is and is not incest, in that Moll does not know it is her brother at the time of commitment, and it is blurred a little by the fact that they have different fathers. As usual, Moll gets away with it, despite all her protestations, in contrast to her poor husband who goes mad with the thought. She goes on to fight another day and finally to be reconciled with the son, and through him, her estate, in Virginia. Moll ends a gentlewoman, shaping her own tale as usual.

Defoe certainly has his dark side. He was a spy, and politically he spent much of his life working and writing anonymously. As the pamphleteer we quoted above suggested, many saw Defoe as a 'true-bred Hypocrite; an High-Church Man one day, and a Rank Whig the next'. He delighted in gulling people and is said to have cheated even his mother-in-law out of money. He went bankrupt several times leaving his wife and family to the charity of relatives. Unlike Moll, he does not end well. Pursued through the courts, yet again, by the widow of a creditor, Mary Brooke, he is forced into hiding. His last surviving letter is distressing, or at least presents someone in distressing circumstances. You never know with Defoe. He describes himself as ill and cut off from any support: 'I have not seen Son or Daughter, Wife or Child, many weeks, and kno' not which way to see them'.[316] This fate is hauntingly presaged in the *Essay upon Projects* written 34 years earlier:

Man is the worst of all creatures to shift for himself; no other animal is ever starved to death; nature without has provided them with food and clothes, and nature within has placed an instinct that never fails to direct them to proper means for a supply; but man must either work, or starve; slave, or die. He has indeed reason given him to direct him, and few who follow the dictates of that reason come to such unhappy exigencies; but when by the errors of a man's youth he has reduced himself to such a degree of distress as to be absolutely without three things – money, friends, and health – he dies in a ditch, or in some worse place, a hospital.[317]

Paterson also dies alone, probably in Westminster, without heirs and somewhat embittered; his second wife and child sacrificed to his Darien adventure. There is a myth around the Bank of England that he became an alcoholic and died in poverty, though there appears to be no evidence to support this.

The figure of the projector is full of ambivalences that put the projector at risk. The project threatens to use up the projector in much the way that we have described a form of writing that uses the writer as a channel and threatens their destruction. The heroic promise of the projector can never be finally fulfilled because the promise, the vision and the audacious plan are what matters. The adventure is itself the motive and the answer. Even now the entrepreneur – despite their domestication since Thatcher and Reagan's 1970s – is a figure who necessarily carries deep ambivalences, provoking admiration and fear, love and distaste. The projector has to manage these ambivalences, embodying the tensions between deceit and honesty, arrogance and determination, the genius and the upstart, as well as being both savior and villain. The projector both projects and is projected, is subject and object of their tale, from which they must be severed in order that their creations can live on after them. We will now explore the implications of this diagnosis in the final chapter of our story, in which you and we and they are all entangled.

Conclusion:
The Projected and Projecting Reader

'An Undertaking Advantagious for the *Publick Good,* Charitable *to the* Poor *and* Profitable *to every Person who shall be concerned therein.'*
(Promotional literature for Henry Mackworth's 'The Governor and Company of the Mine Adventurers of England', in 1699)[318]

The individual reader of the novel is figured by the text of *Moll Flanders* and, we would suggest, by the text of novels in general, as upstanding and intelligent, with the capacity to communicate with the author, and to be in on the secret. Just like you, gentle reader. The preface to *Moll*, as discussed earlier, assumes an already moral audience who can handle a tale about immoral behavior without becoming corrupted themselves. However, there are less able readers around, it suggests by implication, who could be corrupted and are not really worthy of the text. Perhaps there are parallels here with the participant in the organization. The worthy employee and the loyal customer only make sense if we also imagine workers who don't care and shoppers who like to shop around. The general point is that novels and organizations project themselves and those who 'read' them, and in so doing, construct an institution that denies its contingent nature. The ontology of the novel and the Bank as impersonal objects with their own stories to realize negates the author or the founder, and casts the reader, employee, investor or customer as an audience for something that already exists.

Elliot Jaques, an organizational psychologist, suggests that we always need to imagine ourselves as separate from organizations. He describes them as:

An interconnected system of roles with explicit or implicit mutual accountabilities and authorities ... All human relationships take place within such role relationships. Some form of organization must be explicitly established, or at least implicitly assumed, before it becomes possible for people to bring themselves or others into relationships with each other by means of taking up roles in the organization. In other words, organizations have to exist in their own right before people can collect in them.[319]

The paradox is that the audience, while projecting the novel or the organization, must also stand outside it, separate from it, in order for it to exist as a thing in itself. At the same time, the reader of the novel and the participants in organizations are under threat of annihilation by the projections in which they participate. Their discrete identity is threatened by the danger of becoming merely a figure projected by the narrative – a character, employee, reader, manager. In order to be themselves, they must dissent in many small ways from the authority of the novel or of the organization. These are small escape attempts which allow for different readings of any novel, or maintain a sense that they are not merely shadows projected by some other paramount authority.[320] This means that the reader, employee or investor double deals as much as anyone else, practicing their own brand of deceit in that they pretend to believe in the project in order that it may exist while holding themselves at one remove, ready to disengage if necessary and then claim that this has all been 'pretence'. The reader or participant in an organization is normally aware of the illusion but 'pretends' to believe, gives credit, perhaps to fulfil their own needs in dealing with uncertainty and anxiety, or simply because if they ceased to believe, it would cease to exist. And if the story ceases to exist, then perhaps we, as the characters, might cease to exist too.

What do you need to believe in order to make this book work?

Not that much, compared to your average novel or corporation, which usually requires much more credulity. All you really need to do is to grant the text authority, the authority of the story and the lengthy list of endnotes that simulate scholarship and demand to be given credibility. This narrative, the story we tell in this book, is an echo of Defoe's tale of himself and his protagonists. It is about novels, and life, and business, told through the particular story of the intertwining lives of Defoe and Paterson. We have presented evidence that they had very similar characteristics which in turn seem to be inherited by their projects, and so underline the similarities between the novel and the organization. We have also insisted that Defoe's account of the projector is complex rather than simply heroic, carrying ironies and ambivalences. The projector necessarily employs the dark arts, and is always under threat of being used up by the project, a sorcerer's apprentice who is consumed by the magic that he plays with.

So what has this project achieved? The project that has become this book, written by a PhD student and her supervisor three hundred years after Defoe? What has it revealed that was not known or understood before? What contribution will it make to knowledge? Some readers may even want to ask what practical use will it be? These questions have insinuated themselves from the first, whispering 'so what?' So what if a novel is like an organization? What relevance do Defoe and Paterson have to the busy business world of today, or the academic disciplines of the contemporary university? Whilst we value highly the premise that an interesting journey is always worth taking, and a too-tightly-bounded destination would be a betrayal to the projecting nature of the book, we feel that we must say something about the results of our enquiry to satisfy those who require a bottom line. After all, success sanctifies projects.

For a start, we think this story opens up the question of beginnings, in this case, of commercial organizations. We would like to see an account of the origins of the modern organization to compare with the work on the origins of the novel by writers such as Ian Watts, Michael McKeon and John Richetti. Although there has been a great deal of interest in attempts to understand contemporary organization, whether from the Business School, sociology, economics or whatever, there has been very little interest directed at understanding the generic beginnings of the organization. Of course this partly depends on how we define 'an organization', and how that differs from terms such as institution, establishment, corporation, company, firm and so on. Organizations did not begin in the seventeenth century after all, though the specifically corporate form certainly has its beginnings around that time. Nonetheless, this study draws out the paradoxical and contradictory nature of all organizations – whether corporations, states, churches or armies. It suggests that an organization requires to be understood as an impersonal object in order to function as an organization, but also draws out the fictionality of organizations which are shown to be projections in exactly the same way that novels are projections. If we stop believing in them, they cease to exist and only empty buildings and abandoned furnishings are left behind.

It is a primary condition of any organization that it be seen as an impersonal object, a thing with an autonomous existence which stands apart from that of the participants. This primary condition is held in imperfect equilibrium by the equally unassailable fact that the 'objective' nature of the organization or the novel is a deceit, a lie. In accepting the invitation to the fictional projection of the novel or the Bank, we agree to the contract that denies its fictionality. The term 'projection of the organization' is helpful in imagining the simultaneously fictional and objective nature of any social arrangement which starts to become institutionalized. Like the projection of light upon a surface, it is something and nothing, a reality that cannot be grasped, a zoetrope that shows life when it is merely flickering shadow. This characterization raises the issue of transparency in organizations, a demand made by those who wish to insist – quite correctly – on the need for ethical governance and public accountability.

The situation where an organization requires a certain level of deceit and fictionality in order to function becomes problematic under demands for transparency. Indeed, perhaps all organizations require secrecy as a condition of being understood as bounded, as discrete entities which function in distinct ways. That suggests that the stories we tell about organizations tend to construct boundaries, distinctions which themselves produce insides and outsides, those in the know and those who are the audience. We tend to deny the fictional nature of organizations like the Bank of England, insisting on its material and human solidity, and thus deny any hint of deceit or trickery in its very constitution. This leads to periodic outrage when the Bank actually has to employ some necessary deceit to maintain the various fictions it sustains, allegedly for the public benefit. In 2007 the Bank tried to avoid revealing whether and how much it was being asked to lend the failing Northern Rock Bank in order not to encourage a run on that particular bank. Rules of 'transparency' demanded one response while protecting the existing monetary system of the UK required another. The Bank later had to have new legislation drafted in regard to its own requirements to disclose this type of information.[321] There has again been an outcry when in 2012 Paul Tucker, the then-Deputy Governor of the Bank, was reported to have had communications with Bob Diamond, the then-Chief Executive of Barclays. Diamond was accused of trying to fix the interbank lending rate in order to avoid a fall in the price of Barclays' shares which may have discouraged the purchase of those shares by foreign investors from Qatar.[322] Such a collapse in the share price of a major bank would have, again, threatened the stability of the UK financial system. To prevent promises from collapsing, secrecy seems to be required.

So it might be that asking Banks to be transparent is akin to asking a novelist to tell us how she fooled us into believing the story – it rather spoils the point. Of course there is a question of degree here, of the quality of the risk and the extent of the deceit, but as Defoe pointed out in the *Essay upon Projects*, some of the most hazardous projects are favored by fortune and it would be a sin to disallow them. If Henry Mackworth's 'Mine Adventure' of our epigraph to this chapter had succeeded, as all the newspaper articles and handbills of the time suggested it would, we would remember him now as a hero. In fact, that adventure, like so many others, was a disaster which is recalled only by historians, and was attacked at the time for being driven by 'Projectors that have Fiction for their foundation', and its 'Publick-spiritedness, they declared, was merely 'pretended'.[323] Of course it was, because organizations always have fiction as their foundation. We might not be able to see an organization, but that does not mean that they are, or can be, completely transparent. They are always gambles, built on hopeful promises. If we shouted every time we saw the Emperor without any clothes, we would spend a lot of time shouting. But that doesn't mean that we should never draw attention to some of the consequences of organizations exploiting their shape-shifting and fictional nature.

One of the ethical or political consequences of the generic status of an organization as an impersonal fiction is clearly demonstrated in legal attempts to define the corporation and hold it responsible. For example, consider the Bhopal disaster in India in 1984.[324] Twenty-seven tonnes of a gas much more deadly than cyanide leaked from a factory exposing over half a million people to the toxins. An estimated 16 thousand people have died. The owner of the factory, Union Carbide India (UCIL), was half owned by the Union Carbide Corporation (UCC) of the USA, with Indian investment controlling the other half. In 1994, UCC sold its stake in UCIL to Eveready Industries India Limited which then merged with McLeod Russel (India) Ltd. Eveready ended clean-up on the site in 1998, when it terminated its lease and turned the site over to the state government of Madhya Pradesh. Dow Chemical Company purchased UCC in 2001, seventeen years after the disaster. No wonder then that it wasn't until 2010 that seven UCIL managers were found guilty. No-one from UCC has been held responsible, and Dow now denies any liability since it is a different organization, headquartered in Michigan and so not liable to Indian law. The spectral status of the corporation has allowed this organization to shape shift, transferring agency, location and ownership as required. It is its fictional nature that allows for this, since it can appear when there are benefits to solidity, and disappear into the shadows when there are risks or costs to be borne.

Organizations are projections. Plays of shadow and light with real consequences. This situation returns us to the question, in less deadly measure of course, of who is projecting the Bank of England or *Moll Flanders*. Who is writing? In these originating models the 'Good Credit' of the people involved contributed directly to notions of responsibility, not least in that the Directors of the Bank had to invest their own money, as did the printer and the bookseller for a novel. Defoe and Paterson were often enough reminded about the consequences of the failure of projects, but that didn't stop them from projecting again. In some sense, this is because some failure is a necessary consequence of gambling, and their bets were about whether it was possible to produce something impersonal, something that stood outside them but that delivered private benefit and public good.

The impersonal, objective status of the corporation is revolutionary in the early eighteenth century. The Bank was part of the Glorious Revolution that took place in the latter decades of the seventeenth century in England. The impersonal at this moment meant a move towards freedom, away from aristocratic and royal ownership and towards autonomy. This was, for some, a step away from the sort of feudalism which demands that all people are set in their places by birth and marriage. Instead we are here witnessing a moment in which improbable gambles are becoming possible, great wealth is being made and new institutions are being built. The story of the disreputable aristocrat Christopher Monck who gambles his last money on a Spanish treasure-hunting project led by a sailor from New England characterizes this enormous shift in power, and the Bank is part of this particular story. We can imagine a new world. Ironically, to fulfil these revolutionary objectives the Bank quickly becomes recognizable as a bureaucracy in today's terminology. Joseph Addison, writing in the Spectator in 1701, speaks with pleasure and admiration of the hierarchy and impersonal order established by the Bank: 'I looked into the great hall where the Bank is kept, and was not a little pleased to see the directors, secretaries and clerks ... ranged in their several stations according to the parts they hold in that just and regular economy'.[325] Weber's later analysis of bureaucracy stresses the importance of the sense of the impersonal in the fair and equitable allocation of resources.[326] It's an irony that bureaucracy has become a metaphor for sclerotic predictability, when it is necessarily housed within such insecure gambles.

Indeed, to 'call someone a "bureaucrat" is to suggest that they have myopically substituted means for ends, to say that they are strangling themselves and others with red tape, and that (as Eichmann famously argued at his trial) they are only following orders'.[327] Bureaucracy has often been pitted against an 'enterprise culture', promoted by neo-liberals since the 1980s as a way of countering the centralized power of the state.[328] Yet in drawing out the enterprising and revolutionary nature of the Bank, a primary case of a bureaucracy if ever there was one, we are suggesting that this binary opposition is not sustainable. The relationship between enterprise and bureaucracy is a much more complex one. The origins of the project in the seventeenth century, which then become the organization and the bureaucracy, include a movement towards a more equitable distribution of power and resources. The project begins as a challenge to powers earthly and celestial, not an attempt to emplace it in stone and rule from the desk. It is important that this aspect is not forgotten in the ways in which bureaucracy is demonized, when all organizing is politics made durable, and hence potentially revolutionary in its ability to redistribute power and resources.[329] For example, Paul du Gay has drawn attention to the democratic aspects of bureaucracy, the ways in which it offers guarantees to all citizens, without hatred or passion, not just those with noble birth.[330] Organization should not be understood as being only concerned with the protection of power, because it can also be aimed at redistributing and refracting that power, of breaking the monopoly of what counts as common sense in any particular age.

Nowadays, we might understand this in terms of the opposition between enterprise and bureaucracy. The entrepreneur is someone who refuses to rule from the desk, who heroically and tirelessly innovates. Our story suggests something a little different. Not only are bureaucracies based on the suspension of disbelief too, but the entrepreneur is a character occupying and producing a dangerous space. Our exploration of the relationship between the novel and the organization has drawn out the ethical complexities of entrepreneurship because the entrepreneur is someone who necessarily trades in promises. Fictions, necessary deceit, legerdemain and *deceptio visus* are shown to be requirements of the projector – necessary elements in the art of projecting. Current images of the entrepreneur are essentially heroic and lionizing. As the business ethicist John Hendry summarises:

> The components of this entrepreneurial identity naturally vary according to the context, but only slightly. They generally

include such properties as self-reliance, self-motivation, autonomy, personal responsibility, self-regulation, boldness, energy, productivity, efficiency, competitiveness, initiative, innovativeness, creativity, and a willingness to take risks in pursuit of goals...[331]

This is a remarkable set of traits, and it might be noted just how close they come to descriptions of the lionized outlaw too, the criminal whose entrepreneurialism is driven by an impatience with the present.[332] Jones and Spicer have underlined the mythic qualities of this identity, unmasking it as 'a sublime object', both feared and desired.[333] It seems that the predecessor of this figure emerges during the seventeenth century, and is exemplified in the writing of Defoe and other projectors of the age. We can see it in Defoe's characters, such as Robinson Crusoe, Colonel Jack and Moll Flanders, and also in his presentation of himself in his writing. The figure undoubtedly also calls on heroes from myth and legend – the quest and the treasure – but the transformative shift in values at this time, outlined by Watt and McKeon, significantly alters the figure to suit the modern period. The projector is not descended from the Gods, is not repeating past stories, but is creating a new story oriented to the future, with the individual imagination as its fulcrum.

This figure of the entrepreneur inspires fear and admiration, hatred and affection. The ambivalence is caught in the caricature of the piratical entrepreneur as swashbuckling hero, someone with huge creative and destructive potential. A newspaper profile of the British entrepreneur, Philip Green, documents his tendency to lose his temper. 'I just thought you should know', he reportedly told a journalist he disliked, 'I tore your f—ing article out and put it under my cat's arse where it belongs'.[334] Similar stories are often told about entrepreneurs with feet of clay, who hide their avarice behind crocodile smiles and complex layers of offshore holding companies: Maxwell, Branson, Jobs. There is a constant tension between the heroic figure called forth to save the nation from economic hardship and the equally persistent suspicion that he (usually a he) will turn out to be a swindler or, at the very least, of the 'lower orders' with the morals of a market-stall holder, not a gentleman. Moll tells us that 'many a *Newgate* Bird becomes a great Man', and the reverse is also true. This is the same tension established in Defoe's essay with regard to the 'honest' and the 'contemptible' projector. Defoe does not resolve the tension. His paper is merely an 'essay' upon projects; the 'upon' confirming that it can only be an attempt, a try, at understanding the complexities and ironies of the 'art of projecting'.[335] We might need the projector, but they might well let us down.

Approaching Defoe alongside Paterson provides a new perspective on the author's role in the emergence of the novel. It allows us to view him as the projector of the novel, and the novel as a project in itself. Defoe is both object and subject of the project, the author who projects and the author who is projected. Establishing these sorts of equivalences between the Bank and *Moll Flanders* also calls into question the nature and purpose of the novel. In the last century, literature has sought to paint itself as distinctive and special. Literary theory has often suggested that Literature (capitalized) inhabits a space which is sacrosanct and different, somehow morally superior or detached from the commercial world. It is presented as if only the 'space of literature' has the freedom to say anything, and in terms of radical theory, promotes the 'democracy to come'. We aren't so sure about the iconoclastic nature of this characterization and suggest instead that the organization, the beginning of which is always a project, inhabits that space to the same degree as the novel or 'literature' more generally. Art is not our salvation, and the novel is not lord of the space of democracy. Such supposed examples of creativity sustain an establishment to the same degree and in the same ways as the organization because the 'editing pen' is not so far from 'the Governor', and the reader from the employee. The organization must begin with an emancipatory force which unlocks and re-orders power and possibility, though it may develop into the predictability of bureaucracy. So must the novel build a new world, but in so doing, it enters the economy of printers, editors, prizes and money, and its world becomes set in type.

Organizations are made, established, they are not found. Anne Murphy has looked in detail at the practicalities addressed by the Bank of England as it opened in 1694. The minutes of the Directors' meetings record in wonderful detail the problems they confronted and how they were resolved. The Bank had no procedures for the recruitment or management of the tellers for example. It is noted that 'Edward Miller who was chosen this morning for a Teller gives his thanks to the Court, and desires to be excused, by reason he has not been much used to tell money, whereupon James Downes was chosen Teller'.[336] As Murphy notes, 'By 1704 the tellers' duties and responsibilities were codified in a four page set of "Orders for the Observance of the Tellers of the Bank", [which] give the impression of an ordered and hierarchical environment in the banking hall and make it clear that, by this time, there was a strong system of oversight at the Bank of England'. She argues that 'the decisions taken, procedures implemented and mistakes made in the management of the Bank of England's first tellers can reveal much about early modern business practices and can offer new insights into the progress of England's financial revolution'.[337] We catch a glimpse here of actions becoming routines, of bureaucracy being built from a foundation of promises, of models of organization congealing into lumps, like butter from milk. Most of the time, we confront organizations as if they were finished things, established parts of an establishment, complete sets of rules and roles. Our story reminds us that every organized world begins with a fiction, with promises of money and power which are only real if providence smiles upon them, and if enough people believe. Understanding the fictionality of organizations has important consequences for management too since it suggests that there is a strong element of both understanding a narrative at work and being able to tell the tale effectively. The story of the Bank presented here draws out the accidental and the uncanny in its emergence. It was born from high-risk enterprise, uncanny good luck, chutzpah and sheer accident, combined with the canny determination of a series of projectors, foremost among them Paterson, Montague and Godfrey. *Moll Flanders* and the Bank of England share primary conditions and numerous characteristics. They are implicated in each other's development and studying them together has brought out entanglements that were previously unrecognized, such as the potential influence of Paterson on Defoe's fiction, or the importance of storytelling for the foundation of the Bank.

It is likely that other comparisons of this sort could prove fruitful too. How do Restoration Comedies link to the ideas about projection and the novel that we have explored here? Is there a connection between 'gothic' literature and the rise of the industrial factory, and of industrialized printing? Did Anthony Trollope's long career in the Post Office shape his novels, and his attitude towards earning a living from writing? Interdisciplinary work of this kind, asking questions that seem foolish or trivial at first glance, might provide some understanding of the shifting operations of the imagination in different periods of time. It might also tell us something about the commercial arrangements that have influenced the project of both the novel and the organization at particular moments and in particular places. The commercial and the cultural are not opposed, but always entwined. The arguments we have made here regarding the novel, the organization, projecting and projectors, indicate that it is well worth crossing the divide between the disciplines of literary theory and management. This is a recent divide anyway, one made by 'meer scholars' and their institutions in the last century, and not one that would have been recognized by Defoe or Paterson. As Nicholson suggests, 'the intertextuality discovered with the force of revelation in late twentieth-century critical theory is for this political culture [the early eighteenth century] part of an assumed pattern of cross-discursive identification'.[338] This book has merely remembered that fact and fiction are made in the same moment, and hence put back together what we have dismembered.

This book is bad literary theory, bad organization theory, and probably bad history too, because it crosses too many academic boundaries. It might also be bad for the publisher and the bookseller, if they can't find a way to classify it as one thing or another, and hence sell it into a market that will recognize it. Writing always imagines an audience, whether investor, subscriber, purchaser or critic. The same is true within universities, despite much bluster about interdisciplinarity. As Robert Cooper observes:

> The key issue here is the status of writing (including representing) and how it is dealt with in the academic system. The function of the academic division of labour and its representational discourse is to police the effects of writing – undecidability, metaphorization – by maintaining the distinctions between disciplines and the order within them. It is this moral economy of good behaviour that is taught and reproduced in research rather than the quest for enlightenment and truth with which the university is traditionally associated.[339]

Cooper quotes Derrida in support: 'Naturally destined to serve the communication of laws and the order of the city transparently, writing becomes the instrument of an abusive power, of a caste of "intellectuals" that is thus ensuring hegemony, whether its own or that of special interests'. Writing is never innocent, never merely a story. That includes us, of course, your disarmingly honest and reflexive authors. In order to draw the reader into a direct relationship with us that binds them to the tale we present ourselves as honest, just as Defoe presents himself in the Preface to *Moll* and to the *Essay*, and as Moll herself does in the opening pages of her story. We are all going to tell a true tale, one written from memorandums that came into our possession. This is a tale that we hope seduces the reader and encourages you to invest credit in us. (Just as our publisher doubtless hopes the same, with their alchemy of sales figures, pages and prices.) Promises are made. We connect our tale with established authorities: Wordsworth, Marx, Derrida and others. We insinuate too that this is a noble enterprise, in which we are all involved, authors and readers, each drawing sustenance from the other. The reader is approached as 'discerning', a good and 'gentle' person. The relationship is in some ways a bid for a sort of freedom on all our parts, a suggestion that we can make the world anew if you believe in it, if you buy the flickering shadows that we have projected.

This is, of course, a flattering self-image for all of us, one that denies the many ways in which this book can be said to have been written, projected, by Defoe's invisible hand. It is also a book made possible by that moment Abrams pinpoints, in the early eighteenth century, when the concept of the radiant projector took center stage, challenging the idea of the mirror simply reflecting reality.[340] More generally though, writing, of whatever kind, fictional or factual, rational or imaginative, has always been hegemonic in impulse in that it makes worlds. Cooper again draws on Derrida's account of writing, pointing out that it 'grew out of administrative contingencies in the ancient world where it recorded mainly business and statistical information. [Derrida] locates the emergence of formal writing in the agrarian capitalism of the ancient world where it served to stabilize the hierarchical order of "a class that writes or rather commands the scribes" in written balance accounts.'[341]

Writing commands power, and the 'truth' or power of any accounts – fictional, numerical, scientific, realist, reflexive – is highly dependent on any writer's seductive powers. Writing that works, that has effects, spins the reader in a web that entrances and entraps, whether it is a novel written hastily in sections and paid for by the word, a proposal for a project that solicits investment, or a small book about novels and projects. As Rhodes and Brown suggest, in a paper that explores the permeable boundary between fiction and fact in studies of organization:

> ... there is no culture or organization that can be innocently or accurately reflected by researchers. The observer always creates cultural and organisational fictions through the process of their research ... To be self-reflexive implies a preparedness to engage in continual processes of reflection, contest and discovery as we form stories and characters through writing and as we form ourselves in relation to others.[342]

But reflexivity is ultimately just another deceit, another way of pretending to be honest by claiming to be pulling the curtain aside, of producing Realism through a particular sort of simulation. All projects involve the dark arts – promises and projections that can only be fulfilled if you believe in them. After all, our distinctions and puny boundaries are things that we have made, daring projections which rely on credit, and will only keep going if they are thrown well. Hopefully this one has been a good tale, even if the tale is not under our control, or Defoe's, Paterson's or Moll's. Or yours, gentle reader.

Endnotes

1. Quoted in Bronk, Richard. *The Romantic Economist, Imagination in Economics.* Cambridge: University Press, 2009, pvii.

2. Watt, Ian. *The Rise of the Novel 1600-1741.* London: Pimlico, 1957/2000. Nicholson, Colin. *Writing and the Rise of Finance, Capital Satires of the Early Eighteenth Century.* Cambridge: University press, 1994/2004. Gallagher, Catherine. *Nobody's Story: The Vanishing Acts of Women Writers in the Marketplace, 1670-1920.* University of California Press, 1995. Sherman, Sandra. *Finance and Fictionality in the Early Eighteenth century.* Cambridge: University Press, 1996. Poovey, Mary. *Genres of the Credit Economy.* Chicago, IL: University of Chicago Press, 2008. McKeon, Michael. *The Secret History of Domesticity. Public, Private and the Division of Knowledge.* Baltimore, MD; Johns Hopkins University Press, 2009._

3. Haiven, Max. *Cultures of Financialization: Fictitious Capital in Popular Culture and Everyday Life.* London: Palgrave, 2014.

4. Nicholson, Colin. *Writing and the Rise of Finance, Capital Satires of the Early Eighteenth Century,* Cambridge: Cambridge University Press, 1994/2004, p12.

5. Clapham, Sir John. *The Bank of England, Volume 1.* Cambridge: University press, 1944, p14.

6. Defoe, Daniel. *An Essay upon Projects.* London: Bibliobazaar, 1697/2008, p29.

7. Ibid. p26.

8. Ibid, p26.

9. Nicholson, Colin. *Writing and the Rise of Finance, Capital Satires of the Early Eighteenth Century,* Cambridge: Cambridge University Press, 1994/2004, p6.

10. Letter by Defoe signed 'Anti-Pope', published in *Applebee's Journal* 1725, quoted in Watt, Ian. *The Rise of the Novel 1600-*

1741, London: Pimlico, 2000.

11. Novak, Maximillian E. 'Some Notes towards a History of Fictional Forms: from Aphra Behn to Daniel Defoe.' *NOVEL: A Forum on Fiction.* 6/2: 120-133, 1973, p123.

12. Op cit, p32.

13. Yamamoto, Koji. 'Reformation and the Distrust of the Projector in the Hartlib Circle.' *The Historical Journal* 55/2: 375-397, 2012. See also Koji Yamamoto, 'Piety, Profit and Public Service in the Financial Revolution,' *English Historical Review* CXXVI/521: 806-834, 2011.

14. Op cit, p23.

15. Williams, Raymond. 'Realism and the Contemporary Novel.' *Universities & Left Review*, 4, 1958, p22.

16. Doody, Margaret Anne. *The True Story of the Novel.* London: Harper Collins, 1997.

17. Williams, Raymond. 'The Future Story as Formula Novel'. Reprinted in Andrew Milner (ed) *Tenses of Imagination*. Bern: Peter Lang, 2010, p48.

18. See Watt's *The Rise of the Novel*, McKeon's *The Origins of the English Novel*, Forster's *Aspects of the English Novel* and Richetti's *The Modern English Novel*.

19. Lynch, Deirdre and Wil Warner, William B, (eds) *Cultural Institutions of the Novel.* London: Duke University Press, 1996, p2.

20. Parker, Martin *Alternative Business: Outlaws, Crime and Culture.* London: Routledge, 2012.

21. 'Defoe', *The Common Reader*. Quoted in Watt, Ian. *The Rise of the Novel 1600-1741*, London: Pimlico, 2000, p93.

22. Defoe, Daniel. *Robinson Crusoe.* Oxford: University Press, 1998 (1719).

23. Watt, Ian. *The Rise of the Novel 1600-1741*, London: Pimlico, 2000, p94.

24. Defoe, Daniel. *Moll Flanders*, Oxford: University Press, 1971(1722), p273.

25. Ibid. p11.
26. Ibid. pxvi.
27. Guiseppi, John. *The Bank of England*. London: Evan Brothers Ltd., 1966, p12.
28. Roberts, Richard and Kynaston, David eds. *The Bank of England Money, Power and Influence 1694-1994*, Oxford: Clarendon Press, 1995, p1.
29. Campbell, R.H., Skinner, A.S. and Todd, W.B., eds. *Wealth of Nations*. Oxford, 1976, p320.
30. http:www.bankofengland.co.uk/about/Pages/default.aspx. Feb 2013.
31. Williamson, Oliver E. and Winter, Sidney G. *The Nature of the Firm, Origins, Evolution and Development*. Oxford: University Press, 1993, p19.
32. Katz, Jerome and Gartner, William B. 'Properties of Emerging Organizations.' *Academy of Management Review,* 13/3: 429-441, 1988.
33. Pullen, Alison and Rhodes, Carl. 'Borderlines' from *Bits of Organisation*. Eds Alison Pullen and Carl Rhodes. Copenhagen: University Press, 2009, p9.
34. Casson, Mark, *Theory of the Firm*. Cheltenham: Edward Elgar Publishing, 1996, p463.
35. Henderson, A.M., Parsons, Talcott and Weber, Max. *The Theory of Social and Economic Organisation*. London: Free Press: Collier-Macmillan, 1947.
36. Micklethwaite, John and Woolridge, Adrian. *The Company, A Short History of a Revolutionary Idea*. New York: Modern Library, 2005, pxvi.
37. Ibid, p5.
38. Sampson, Alan. *Company Man, The Rise and Fall of Corporate Life*. London: Harper Collins, 1996, p16.
39. Op cit, p54.
40. Bronk, Richard. *The Romantic Economist, Imagination in Economics*. Cambridge: University Press, 2009, p18.

41. Ibid. p19.
42. Watt, Ian. *The Rise of the Novel 1600-1741*, London: Pimlico, 2000, p9.
43. Hunter, J. Paul. 'Serious Reflections on Daniel Defoe (with an Excursus on the Farther Adventures of Ian Watt and two notes on the Present State of Literary Studies).' *Eighteenth Century Fiction* 12/2-3: 227-238, 2000.
44. Watt, Ian. *The Rise of the Novel 1600-1741*, London: Pimlico, 2000, p9.
45. Meyer, Robert. *History and the early English Novel.* Cambridge: University Press, 1997, p181.
46. Clark, Timothy. *The Theory of Inspiration.* Manchester: University Press, 1997, p1.
47. Kamuf, Peggy (ed. and trans.) *A Derrida Reader, Between the Blinds.* London: Harvester Wheatsheaf, 1991.
48. Clark, Timothy. *The Theory of Inspiration.* Manchester: University Press, 1997, p5.
49. Ibid. p15.
50. Ibid. pp10-11.
51. Novak, Maximillian E (ed.) *The Age of Projects.* Toronto: University of Toronto Press, 2008.
52. Defoe, Daniel. *An Essay upon Projects.* London: Bibliobazaar, 2008 (1697), p21.
53. Ibid. p21.
54. Mokyr, Joel, *The Enlightened Economy, An Economic History of Britain from 1700-1850* Yale, 2009, p23.
55. Ibid. p3.
56. Novak, Maximillian E. 'Some Notes towards a History of Fictional Forms: From Aphra Behn to Daniel Defoe,' *NOVEL: A Forum on Fiction.* 6/2: 120-133, 1973, p123.
57. Clark, Timothy. *Derrida, Heidegger, Blanchot.* Cambridge: University Press, 1992.
58. Parker, M. 'Organization and Philosophy: Vision and Division.' In R. Mir, H. Willmott and M. Greenwood (eds),

Companion to Philosophy in Organization Studies. London: Routledge, 2015.

59. Abrahms, M.H. *The Mirror and the Lamp. Romantic Theory and the Critical Tradition.* Oxford: University Press, 1953/1977.

60. Lodge, David, ed. *Twentieth Century Literary Criticism, A Reader.* Essex: Longman, 1972, p1.

61. Pocock, J.G.A. *The Machiavellian Moment.* London: Princeton University Press. 1975.

62. Nicholson, Colin. *Writing and the Rise of Finance, Capital Satires of the Early Eighteenth Century,* Cambridge: University Press, 1994/2004, p5.

63. Ingrassia, Catherine. *Authorship, Commerce and Gender in early eighteenth-century England.* Cambridge: University Press, 1998, p5.

64. Ibid. p2.

65. Sherman, Sandra. *Finance and Fictionality in the early 18th Century: Accounting for Defoe.* Cambridge: University Press, 1996.

66. Ibid. p14

67. Minto, William, *Daniel Defoe.* London: Macmillan, 1879 quoted in Novak, Maximillian, *Daniel Defoe, Master of Fictions,* Oxford: University Press, 2003, p2.

68. McKeon, Michael. *The Origins of the Novel 1600-1741.* Baltimore: The John Hopkins University Press, 2002, p121.

69. Robert, Marthe. *Origins of the Novel.* Brighton: Harvester Press, 1980, p3.

70. Defoe, Daniel. *Moll Flanders,* Oxford: University Press, 1971 (1722), p1.

71. Mayer, Robert. *History and the Early English Novel.* Cambridge: Cambridge University Press, 1992, p192.

72. Ibid. p7.

73. Davies, Paul. Lecture at University of Sussex, 2007.

74. Watt, Ian. *The Rise of the Novel 1600-1741,* London: Pimlico, 2000, p18.

75. Middleton, Thomas and Dekker, Thomas. *The Roaring Girl,* 1607-10. See also Sian Rees, *The Life and Times of Moll Flanders.* London: Pimlico, 2012.

76. Connor, Rebecca Elisabeth. *Women, Accounting and Narrative.* London: Routledge, 2004. p111.

77. Bannister, Saxe. *The Writings of William Paterson Vol 2,* British Library, p66.

78. Paterson, Wiliam. 'A Brief Account of the Intended Bank of England', London, 1694, p5.

79. Bannister, Saxe. 'A Brief Account of the Intended Bank of England', London: Randal Taylor, near Stationers Hall. 1694, p5.

80. Giuseppi, John. *The Bank of England.* London: Evan Brothers Ltd., 1966, p11.

81. Andreades, A. *History of the Bank of England 1640-1903.* London: Frank Cass and Co. Ltd., 1966, p137.

82. Op cit, p2.

83. Op cit, p18.

84. Op cit, p12.

85. Clapham, Sir John. *The Bank of England, Volume 1.* Cambridge: University press, 1944, p20.

86. Ingrassia, Catherine. *Authorship, Commerce and Gender in early eighteenth-century England.* Cambridge: University Press, 1998, p88.

87. Clapham, Sir John. *The Bank of England Vol 1,* Cambridge: University Press, 1944, p24-25.

88. Pincus, Steve. *1688 The First Modern Revolution.* Pennsylvania: Yale, W. Hilles Publications, 2009, p43.

89. Nicholson, Colin. *Writing and the Rise of Finance, Capital Satires of the Early Eighteenth Century,* Cambridge: University Press, 1994/2004, p18. See also Koji Yamamoto, 'Piety, Profit and Public Service in the Financial Revolution,' *English Historical Review* CXXVI/521: 806-834, 2011.

90. Scott, William Robert. *The Constitution and Finance of*

English, Scottish and Irish joint-stock companies to 1720, Volume 1, The General Development of the Joint-stock System to 1720. New York: Peter Smith, 1951, p106.

91. Defoe, Daniel. *An Essay upon Publick Credit.* Quoted in Sherman, Sandra, 'Promises, Promises: credit as Contested Metaphor in Early Capitalist Discourse,' *Modern Philology* Vol. 94, No. 3, Feb 1997, p327.

92. Nicholson, Colin. *Writing and the Rise of Finance, Capital Satires of the Early Eighteenth Century,* Cambridge: University Press, 1994/2004.

93. Olsen, Thomas Grant. 'Reading and Righting Moll Flanders', *Studies in Engish liyerature* 41/3: 467-481.

94. Defoe, Daniel. *Moll Flanders*, Oxford: University Press, 1971 (1722), p1.

95. Ibid. p4.

96. Ibid. p2.

97. Defoe, Daniel. *An Essay upon Projects.* London: Bibliobazaar, 2008 (1697), p13.

98. Clapham, Sir John. *The Bank of England, Volume 1.* Cambridge: University press, 1944, p18.

99. Giuseppi, John. *The Bank of England.* London: Evan Brothers Ltd., 1966, p26.

100. Yamamoto, Koji. 'Piety, Profit and Public Service in the Financial Revolution,' *English Historical Review* CXXVI: 521, p 811, 2011.

101. Acres, W. Marston. *The Bank of England from Within.* London: Oxford University Press, 1931, p22.

102. Acres, W. Marston. 'The First Governor of the Bank' from the magazine *The Old Lady of Threadneedle Street*, Vol. 4, 1927/8, p155.

103. Capie, Forrest. *The Bank of England 1950s to 1979*, Cambridge: University Press, 2010, pxvii.

104. Eliot, T.S. 'Little Gidding V', *Four Quartets*. 1942. Eliot worked at Lloyds Bank from 1917-25.

105. Royle, Nicholas. *Jacques Derrida*. London: Routledge, 2003, p27.

106. Sherman, Sandra. *Finance and Fictionality in the early 18ᵗʰ Century*. Cambridge: University Press, 1996.

107. Pincus, Steve. *1688: The First Modern Revolution*. Pennsylvania: Yale, W. Hilles Publications, 2009, p3.

108. Dickson, P.G.M. The *Financial Revolution in England: A Study in the Development of Public Credit 1688-1756*, London: Macmillan, 1967. Mokyr, Joel. *The Enlightened Economy, An economic history of Britain 1700-1850*, Yale University Press, 2009.

109. Pincus, Steve. *1688: The First Modern Revolution*. Pennsylvania: Yale, W. Hilles Publications, 2009, p31.

110. McKeon, Michael. *The Origins of the Novel 1600-1741*. Baltimore: The John Hopkins University Press, 2002, p159.

111. Mokyr, Joel. *The Enlightened Economy, An Economic History of Britain 1700-1850*. Yale: University Press, 2009, p17.

112. Doepke, Matthias and Zillibetti, Fabrizio, 'Occupational Choice and the Spirit of Capitalism', *Quarterly Journal of Economics*, Vol. 123/2: 747-93, 2008.

113. Ackroyd, Peter. *London, the Biography*, London: Chatto and Windus, 2000, p390.

114. Ibid, p390.

115. Cited in Parker, Martin. *Alternative Business*. London: Routledge, p65, 2012.

116. Ackroyd, op cit.

117. Hay, Douglas, Peter Linebaugh, John G. Rule, E. P. Thompson, and Cal Winslow *Albion's Fatal Tree: Crime and Society in Eighteenth-Century England*. London: Verso, 1975/2011.

118. Novak, Maximillian. *Daniel Defoe, Master of Fictions*, Oxford: University Press, 2003, p537.

119. Ibid, p220.

120. Clark, Timothy. *The Theory of Inspiration*. Manchester:

University Press, 1997, p92.

121. See Ian Watt, Raymond Williams and Jose Ortega y Gasset in McKeon, Michael ed. *Theory of the Novel*. Baltimore: John Hopkins University Press, 2000.

122. Royle, Nicholas. *Jacques Derrida*. London: Routledge, 2004, p45.

123. Robert, Marthe. *Origins of the Novel*. Brighton: Harvester Press, 1980, p32.

124. Eagleton, Terry. *The English Novel, An Introduction*. Oxford: Blackwell Publishing, 2005, p9.

125. Ibid, p17.

126. Pincus, Steve. *1688: The First Modern Revolution*. Pennsylvania: Yale, W. Hilles Publications, 2009, p8.

127. Dickson, P.G.M. *The Financial Revolution in England: A Study in the Development of Public Credit 1688-1756*, London, 1967, p9.

128. Kynaston, David and Roberts, Richard, eds. *The Bank of England, Money, Power and Influence, 1694-1994*. Oxford: University Press, 1995, p2.

129. Paterson, William. 'A Brief Account of the Intended Bank of England, 1694', 1694, p2.

130. Clapham, Sir John. *The Bank of England, Volume 1*. Cambridge: University Press, 1944, p3.

131. Ibid. p4.

132. Ibid. p16.

133. Giuseppi, John. *The Bank of England*. London: Evan Brothers Ltd., 1966, p12

134. Ibid, p9.

135. Clapham, Sir John. *The Bank of England, Volume 1*. Cambridge: University Press, 1944, p15.

136. Giuseppi, John. *The Bank of England*. London: Evan Brothers Ltd., 1966, p88.

137. Acres, Marston W. *The Old Lady, Magazine of the Bank of England*, Vol.4, 1927, p113.

138. Watt, Ian. *The Rise of the Novel 1600-1741*, London: Pimlico, 2000, p57.

139. Shaw, David J. 'Serialization of Moll Flanders in the London Post and the Kentish Post, 1722'. *The Library: The Transactions of the Bibliographic Society*, 8/2: 182-192, 2007.

140. Backscheider, Paula R. *Moll Flanders: The Making of a Criminal Mind*. Boston: Twayne Publishers, 1990, p11.

141. Watt, Ian. *The Rise of the Novel 1600-1741*, London: Pimlico, 2000, p99.

142. Defoe, Daniel. *Moll Flanders*, Oxford: University Press, 1971 (1722), pp59-60.

143. Johns, Adrian. *The Nature of the Book, Print and Knowledge in the Making*. London: Chicago Press, 1998.

144. Defoe, Daniel. *Moll Flanders*, Oxford: University Press, 1971 (1722), ppxxiv-xxv.

145. Forrester, Andrew. *The Man who Saw the Future*. US: Thomson, 2004, p309.

146. Paterson, William. 'A Brief Account of the Intended Bank of England', 1694, E. Huntingdon Library and Art Gallery, *EEBO*, 2012.

147. Carlos, Ann M. and Neal, Larry. 'The micro-foundations of the early London capital market: Bank of England Shareholders during and after the South Sea Bubble, 1720-25,' *Economic History Review*, 59/3: 498-538, 2006, p498.

148. Watt, Ian. *The Rise of the Novel 1600-1741*, London: Pimlico, 2000, p36.

149. www.pepys.info/661/661feb.html

150. Novak, Maximillian. *Daniel Defoe, Master of Fictions*, Oxford: University Press, 2003, p307.

151. Jackson, Ian. 'Approaches to the History of Readers and Reading in Eighteenth Century Britain' *Historiographical Review*, 47/4: 1041-1054, 2004, p1047.

152. Watt, Ian. *The Rise of the Novel 1600-1741*, London: Pimlico, 2000, p42.

153. Pincus, Steve. *1688: The First Modern Revolution.* Pennsylvania: Yale, W. Hilles Publications, 2009, p81.

154. Ibid., p59.

155. Forrester, Andrew. *The Man who Saw the Future.* US: Thomson, 2004, p59.

156. Ibid, p63.

157. Andreades, A. *History of the Bank of England 1640-1903.* London: Frank Cass and Co. Ltd., 1966, p61.

158. Calhoun, Craig. 'Introduction', *Habermas and the Public Sphere.* Cambridge MA: MIT Press, 1992.

159. Barrell, John. 'Coffee-house Politicians', *Journal of British Studies.* Vol.43. No.2, 206-232, 2004.

160. Hunter, J.Paul. '"News and New Things": Contemporaneity and the Early English Novel,' *Critical Inquiry,* Vol.14, No.3, 493-515, 1998.

161. Pincus, Steve. *1688: The First Modern Revolution.* Pennsylvania: Yale, W. Hilles Publications, 2009, p259.

162. Defoe, Daniel. *Moll Flanders,* Oxford: University Press, 1971 (1722), p11.

163. Hammond, Brean S. *Professional Imaginative Writing In England 1670-1740, 'Hackney for Bread'.* Oxford: Clarendon Press. 1997.

164. Foxon, David. *Pope and the Early Eighteenth Century Book Trade,* Oxford: Clarendon Press, 1991.

165. Ibid, p4.

166. Stephen, Leslie. *English Literature and Society in the Eighteenth Century,* London, 1963, p.51.

167. Ibid, p6.

168. Nicholson, Colin. *Writing and the Rise of Finance, Capital Satires of the Early Eighteenth Century,* Cambridge: University Press, 1994/2004.

169. Defoe, Daniel. *Moll Flanders,* Oxford: University Press, 1971(1722), pxvii.

170. Novak, Maximillian. *Daniel Defoe, Master of Fictions,* Oxford:

University Press, 2003, p565.

171. Ibid, p45.
172. Ingrassia, Catherine. *Authorship, Commerce and Gender in early eighteenth-century England.* Cambridge: University Press, 1998, p1.
173. Nicholson, Colin. *Writing and the Rise of Finance, Capital Satires of the Early Eighteenth Century,* Cambridge: University Press, 1994/2004, pxi.
174. Bellamy, Liz. *Commerce, Morality and the eighteenth century novel,* Cambridge: University Press, 1998, p15.
175. Pocock, J.G.A. 'The Mobility of Property and the Rise of eighteenth century Sociology', *Virtue, Commerce and History: Essays on Political Thought and History,* Cambridge, 1985. Quoted in Ingrassia, Catherine. *Authorship, Commerce and Gender in early eighteenth- century England.* Cambridge: University Press, 1998, p3.
176. Defoe, Daniel. *A Hymn to the Pillory,* in Shakespeare Head Edition, 138-9, quoted in Maximillian Novak, *Daniel Defoe, Master of Fictions,* Oxford: University Press, 2003, p193.
177. Novak, Maximillian. *Daniel Defoe, Master of Fictions.,* Oxford: University Press, 2003, p193.
178. Giuseppi, John. *The Bank of England.* London: Evan Brothers Ltd., 1966, p88.
179. Defoe, Daniel. *Moll Flanders,* Oxford: University Press, 1971(1722), p1.
180. McKeon, Michael. *The Origins of the Novel 1600-1741.* Baltimore: The John Hopkins University Press, 2002, p167.
181. Rabinow, Paul. (ed.) *The Foucault Reader, An Introduction to Foucault's Thought.* London: Penguin, 1991, p103.
182. Op cit, p83.
183. Op cit, p123.
184. Bank of England Act 1694 (c.20) p1.
    http://www.statutelaw.gov.ukcontent.aspn?legType=All-Primary&page Number=1.

185. Ibid. p3.

186. http://www.bankofengland.co.uk/about/Document/legis-lation/1694charter.

187. Roberts, Richard and Kynaston, David (eds.) *The Bank of England, Money, Power and Influence 1694-1994.* Clarendon Press, 1995, p217.

188. Sampson, Anthony. *Company Man. The Rise and Fall of Corporate Life,* London: Harper Collins, 1995, p78.

189. Veldman, J and Parker, M 'Specters, Inc.: The Evasive Basis of the Corporation' *Business and Society Review* 117/4: 413-441, 2012.

190. Defoe, Daniel. *Moll Flanders,* Oxford: University Press, 1971 (1722), p1.

191. Rabinow, Paul (ed.) *The Foucault Reader, An Introduction to Foucault's Thought.* London: Penguin, 1991, p103.

192. Connor, Rebecca Elisabeth. *Women, Accounting and Narrative.* London: Routledge, 2004, p148.

193. www.BankofEngland.co.uk/about/pages/default.aspx.

194. Bannister, Saxe. (ed.) *The Writings of William Paterson,* 1858. Preface. British Library.

195. Boyer's Political State 1711, 2nd Edition, p1.

196. Derrida, Jacques. 'Some Statements and Truisms about Neologisms, Newisms, Postisms, Parasitisms, and other Small Seismisms.' In David Carroll (ed.), *The States of Theory,* New York: Columbia University Press, 1989, p65.

197. Rogers, Pat. *Grub Street: Studies in a Subculture.* London: Methuen and Co. Ltd., 1972.

198. Novak, Maximillian. *Daniel Defoe, Master of Fictions,* Oxford: University Press, 2003, p597.

199. Clark, Timothy. *The Theory of Inspiration.* Manchester: University Press, 1997, p23.

200. Brant, Clare and Purkiss, Diane (eds.), *Women, Texts and Histories 1575-1760.* London: Routledge, 1992, p164. See also Sian Rees, *The Life and Times of Moll Flanders.* London:

Pimlico, 2012.

201. Berry, Helen. 'Rethinking Politeness in Eighteenth Century England: Moll King's Coffee House and the significance of "Flash Talk".' *Royal Historical Society, Sixth Series,* 11: 65-81, 2001. See also Sian Rees, *The Life and Times of Moll Flanders.* London: Pimlico, 2012.

202. Eagleton, Terry. *The English Novel, An Introduction.* Oxford: Blackwell Publishing, 2005, p22.

203. Backscheider, Paula R. *Moll Flanders The making of a Criminal Mind.* Boston: Twayne Publishers, 1990, p2.

204. Forster, E.M. *Aspects of the Novel.* London: Edward Arnold, 1927.

205. Watt, Ian. *The Rise of the Novel 1600-1741,* London: Pimlico, 2000, p115.

206. Clark, Timothy. *The Theory of Inspiration.* Manchester: Manchester University Press, 1997, p242.

207. Macaulay, Thomas Babington. *The History of England.* London: Dent, 1965.

208. Steel, W.A. 'William Paterson' *The English Historical Review,* 11/42: 260-281, 1896, p264.

209. Forrester, Andrew. *The Man who Saw the Future.* US: Thomson, 2004.

210. Capie, Forrest. *The Bank of England 1950-1979.* Cambridge: University Press, 2010, p1.

211. Clapham, Sir John. *The Bank of England, A History, Volume 1 1694-1797.* Cambridge: University Press, 1944, p1.

212. *Gesammelte Werke* quoted in 'The Houses of Fiction: Toward a Definition of the Uncanny'. Maria M. Tatar *Comparative Literature,* Vol.33, No.2 (spring, 1981), pp167-182.

213. Royle, Nicholas. *The Uncanny.* Manchester: University Press, 2003, p1.

214. Ibid. p88.

215. Ibid. p191.

216. A historical mistake, given that the text ends with the claim

that it was 'Written in the Year 1683'.

217. Ibid, p154.

218. Ibid, p152.

219. Ibid, p189.

220. Ibid, p189.

221. Levitt, Carl. 'Defoe's almost Invisible Hand, Narrative Logic as a Structuring Principle' *Eighteenth Century Fiction*, 6/1: 1-28, 1993.

222. Clark, Timothy. *The Theory of Inspiration*. Manchester: University Press, 1997, p26.

223. Ibid. p33.

224. Rabinow, Paul, ed. 'Nietzsche, Genealogy, History' from *The Foucault Reader*, London: Penguin, 1991, p81.

225. Forrester, Andrew. *The Man who Saw the Future*. US: Thomson, 2004, p51.

226. Dickson, P.G.M. *The Financial Revolution in England: A Study in the Development of Public Credit. 1688-1756*. London: Macmillan, 1967, p54.

227. Forrester, op cit, p53.

228. Clapham, John, *The Bank of England*, Vol 1. Cambridge: Cambridge University Press, 1944.

229. Bannister, Saxe. *William Paterson, The Merchant Statesman, and Founder of the Bank of England*. Edinburgh: William P. Nimmo, 1858. Pxxii.

230. Thornton, Mark. 'Cantillon and the Invisible Hand,' *Quarterly Journal of Austrian Economics* 12/2: 27-46, 2009.

231. Macfie, A.L. 'The *Invisible Hand* of Jupiter', *Journal of the History of Ideas*, xxxii (1971), pp595–9.

232. William Shakespeare, *Macbeth*, Act III, Scene II.

233. Macfie, A.L. 'The *Invisible Hand* of Jupiter', *Journal of the History of Ideas*, 32:595–9, 1971.

234. Furbank P.N. and Owens, W.R. 'Defoe and King William: A Sceptical Enquiry', *The Review of English Studies*; 52: 227-232, 2001.

235. Novak, M.E. *Daniel Defoe, Master of Fictions*, Oxford: University Press, 2003, p77.

236. Forrester, Andrew. *The Man who Saw the Future*. US: Thomson, 2004, p7.

237. Ibid, p33.

238. Bannister, Saxe (ed.) *The Writings of William Paterson, Founder of the Bank of England*, 3 vols. British Library.1858. Preface.

239. Op cit, p58.

240. Novak, Maximillian. *Daniel Defoe, Master of Fictions*, Oxford: University Press, 2003, p114.

241. 'Appeal to Honour and Justice', *The Shortest way with Dissenters and Other Pamphlets*. Shakespeare head Edition, 195.

242. Furbank and Owens, op cit, p232.

243. Steel, W.A. 'William Paterson' *The English Historical Review*, 11/42: 260-281, 1896, p264.

244. Armitage, John. 'William Paterson 1658-1719'. *Oxford DNB*. Oxford: University Press, 2004-6.

245. Novak, Maximillian. *Daniel Defoe, Master of Fictions*, Oxford: University Press, 2003, p164.

246. Bannister, Saxe. *William Paterson, The Merchant Statesman, and Founder of the Bank of England. His Life and Trials*, by. Edinburgh: William P Nimmo, MDCCC LVIII. p411.

247. Sutherland, James. *Daniel Defoe*. Cambridge, MA : Harvard University Press,. 1971, p108.

248. Novak, Maximillian. *Daniel Defoe, Master of Fictions*, Oxford: University Press, 2003, p194.

249. Ibid, p302.

250. Ibid. p319.

251. Armitage, David. 'The Projecting Age,' *History Today*, 44/6 : 5-10, 1994.

252. McVeagh, J. ed. Owens and Furbank (eds.) *Defoe Novels Vol 10. New Voyage*. London: Pickering and Chatto, 2009, p4.

253. Novak, Maximillian. *Daniel Defoe, Master of Fictions*, Oxford: University Press, 2003, p310.

254. Backscheider, Paula R. *Daniel Defoe: His Life*. Baltimore and London: The Johns Hopkins University Press, 1989, pxi.

255. Davis, Lennard J. *Factual Fictions, The Origins of the English Novel*. Philadelphia: University of Pennsylvania, 1996. Sutherland, James. *Daniel Defoe*. Cambridge, MA: Harvard University Press, 1971, p255.

256. Richetti, John. *The Life of Daniel Defoe*. Oxford: Blackwell, 2005, p3.

257. Sutherland, James. *Daniel Defoe*. Cambridge: University Press, 1971, p11.

258. Op cit, p4.

259. Novak, Maximillian. *Daniel Defoe, Master of Fictions*, Oxford: University Press, 2003, p70.

260. Armitage, David. 'The Projecting Age,' *History Today*, 44:6 (1994, June).

261. Forrester, Andrew. *The Man who Saw the Future*. US: Thomson, 2004, p15.

262. Ibid. p16.

263. Richetti, John. *England in the Reign of James II and William III*, Oxford: University Press, 1984; first published 1955, pp42-3.

264. Novak, Maximillian. *Daniel Defoe, Master of Fictions*, Oxford: University Press, 2003, p40.

265. Ibid, p48.

266. Ibid, p46.

267. Bannister, Saxe. *The Writings of William Paterson Vol III*. Preface. British Library.

268. Steel, W.A. 'William Paterson,' *The English Historical Review*, 11/42: 260-281, 1896

269. Macaulay, Thomas Babington. *The History of England*. London: Dent, 1965, p466.

270. Clapham, John. *The Bank of England, Vol.1*. Cambridge: University Press. 1944, p14.

271. Bateson, Thomas. 'The Relations of Defoe and Harley', *The English Historical Review*, Vol.15, No.58 (April 1900), pp238-250.

272. Bannister, Saxe, ed. *The Writings of William Paterson, Founder of the Bank of England*, 3 vols. British Library. 1858.

273. Armitage, David. 'William Paterson 1658-1719', Oxforddnb.com.ezproxy.sussex.ac.uk 07/09/2006

274. Richetti, John. *The Life of Daniel Defoe*. Oxford: Blackwell Publishing, 2005, p35.

275. Giuseppi, John. *The Bank of England*. London: Evan Brothers Ltd., 1966, p9.

276. Eagleton, Terry. *The English Novel*, Oxford: Blackwell, 2005, p1-2.

277. Guillen, Claudio, *Literature as System: Essays toward the Theory of Literary History*. Princeton, N.J.: University Press, 1971 quoted in McKeon Michael, (ed.) *Theory of the Novel*. Baltimore: John Hopkins University Press, 2000, p45.

278. Richetti, John. *The Life of Daniel Defoe*. Oxford: Blackwell Publishing 2005, p10.

279. Novak, Maximillian. *Daniel Defoe, Master of Fictions*, Oxford: University Press, 2003, p82.

280. Op cit, p10.

281. Novak, Maximillian. *Daniel Defoe, Master of Fictions*, Oxford: University Press, 2003 p85.

282. Connor, Rebecca Elisabeth. *Women, Accounting and Narrative*. London: Routledge, 2004, p92.

283. Ibid. p92.

284. Novak, Maximillian. *Daniel Defoe, Master of Fictions*, Oxford: University Press, 2003, p99.

285. Ibid. p114.

286. Macaulay, Thomas Babington. *The History of England*. London: Dent, 1965, p477.

287. Forrester, Andrew. *The Man who Saw the Future*. US: Thomson, 2004, p31.

288. Macaulay, Thomas Babington. *The History of England*. London: Dent, 1965, p478.

289. Ibid. p174.

290. Ibid. p481.

291. Ibid. p483.

292. Ibid. p484.

293. Forrester, Andrew. *The Man who Saw the Future*. US: Thomson, 2004.p269.

294. Macaulay, Thomas Babington. *The History of England*. London: Dent, 1965, p487.

295. Steel, W.A. 'William Paterson', *The English Historical Review*, 11/42: 260-281, 1896; Novak, Maximillian. *Daniel Defoe, Master of Fictions*, Oxford: University Press, 2003.

296. Novak, ibid, p607.

297. Novak, ibid, p157.

298. Davis, Lennard J. *Factual Fictions*, Philadelphia: University Press, 1996, p155.

299. Sian Rees. *The Life and Times of Moll Flanders*. London: Pimlico, 2012, p170.

300. Steel, W.A. 'William Paterson', *The English Historical Review*, 11/42: 260-281, 1896

301. Macaulay, Thomas Babington. *The History of England*. London: Dent, 1965, p476.

302. Macaulay. T.B. *The History of England*. Vol 4. London: Everyman's Library, Dent, 1906, p90.

303. Ibid. p14.

304. Ibid. p274.

305. Ibid. p241.

306. Brague, Remi. *The Law of God: The Philosophical History of an Idea*. Chicago: University Press, 2008.

307. Davis, Lennard J. *Factual Fictions, the origins of the English Novel*. Philadelphia: University of Pennsylvania, 1996, p173.

308. Novak, Maximillian. *The Age of Projects*, Toronto: University of Toronto Press, 2008.

309. Mokyr, Joel. *The Enlightened Economy. An Economic History of Britain 1700-1850.* London: Yale University Press, 2009, p13.

310. Lindsay. W.B. 'Defoe's Review – Forerunner of Modern Journalism,' *The English Journal,* 16: 359-363, 1927.

311. Andrews J.H. 'Defoe and the Sources of his "Tour"'. *The Geographical Journal,* 126/3: 268-277, 1960.

312. Casson, Mark. *The Entrepreneur, An Economic Theory.* Oxford: Martin Robertson and Co. Ltd. 1982, p22.

313. Yamamoto, Koji, 'Reformation and the Distrust of the Projector in the Hartlib Circle,' *The Historical Journal* 55/2: 375-397, 2012.

314. Defoe, Daniel. *Moll Flanders,* Oxford: University Press, 1971(1722), p49.

315. Ibid, p174.

316. Richetti, John. *The Life of Daniel Defoe.* Oxford: Blackwell, 2005, p359.

317. Defoe, Daniel. *An Essay upon Projects.* London: Bibliobazaar, 2008 (1697), p34.

318. Yamamoto, Koji. 'Piety, Profit and Public Service in the Financial Revolution,' *English Historical Review* CXXVI: 521: 806-834, 2011, p813.

319. Armstrong, David. 'Emotions in Organizations: Disturbance or Intelligence'. *Working Below the Surface, The Emotional Life of Contemporary Organizations,* Tavistock Clinic Series. London: Karnac, 2007, p21.

320. Cohen, S and Taylor L. *Escape Attempts.* London: Routledge, 1976/1992.

321. See Banking (Special Provisions) Act 2008 which gave the Bank exemption from the Freedom of Information Act 2000 in certain circumstances.

322. It has now been reported in the press that the funds actually came from Abu Dhabi.

323. Yamamoto, op cit, 813.

324. Veldman, Jeroen and Parker, Martin. 'Specters, Inc.: The

Elusive Basis of the Corporation', *Business and Society Review*, 117/4: 413-441, 2012.

325. Geddes, P. *Inside the Bank of England*. London: Boxtree Ltd., 1987, p15.

326. Andreski, Stanislav, ed. *Max Weber and capitalism, bureaucracy and religion: a selection of texts*. London: Allen and Unwin, 1983.

327. Parker, Martin. *Against Management*. Cambridge: Polity Press, 2004, p17.

328. Fournier, Valerie and Grey, Christopher. 'Too Much, Too Little and Too Often: A Critique of du Gay's Analysis of Enterprise'. *Organization* 6/1: 107-128.

329. Parker, M, Cheney, G, Fournier, V, and Land, C (eds) *The Companion to Alternative Organization*. London: Routledge, 2014.

330. Du Gay, Paul. *In Praise of Bureaucracy*. London: Sage, 2000.

331. Hendry, John. 'Cultural confusions of enterprise and the myth of the bureaucratized entrepreneur', *The International Journal of Entrepreneurship and Innovation*, 5/1: 53-57, 2004.

332. Parker, Martin. *Alternative Business: Outlaws. Crime and Culture*. London: Routledge, 2012.

333. Jones, Campbell and Spicer, Andre. *Unmasking the Entrepreneur*. Cheltenham: Edward Elgar, 2009.

334. Lewis, Patricia and Llewellyn, Nick. 'Special Issue: Enterprise and entrepreneurial activity.' *The International Journal of Entrepreneurship and Innovation* 5/1.

335. Defoe, Daniel. *An Essay upon Projects*. London: Bibliobazaar, 2008. (1697)

336. Bank of England Archive G4/1 Records of the Court of Directors July 27th 1694-March 20th 1694, p10.

337. Murphy, Anne L. 'Learning the Business of Banking: The management of the Bank of England's first tellers,' *Business History*, 52/1: 150-168, 2010, p151.

338. Nicholson, Colin. *Writing and the Rise of Finance, Capital*

Satires of the Early Eighteenth Century, Cambridge: University Press, 1994/2004, p10.

339. Cooper, Robert. 'Modernism, Post Modernism and Organizational Analysis 3: The Contribution of Jacques Derrida,' *Organization Studies*, 1989, 10/4 479-502, p495.

340. Abrahms, M. H. *The Mirror and the Lamp, Romantic Theory and the Critical Tradition.* Oxford: University Press, 1953/1977.

341. Derrida quoted in Cooper, op cit, p493.

342. Rhodes, Carl and Brown, Andrew D. (2005) 'Writing Responsibly: Narrative Fiction and Organization Studies,' *Organization* 12/4: 467-49, 2005, p477.

zero
books

Contemporary culture has eliminated both the concept of the public and the figure of the intellectual. Former public spaces – both physical and cultural – are now either derelict or colonized by advertising. A cretinous anti-intellectualism presides, cheerled by expensively educated hacks in the pay of multinational corporations who reassure their bored readers that there is no need to rouse themselves from their interpassive stupor. The informal censorship internalized and propagated by the cultural workers of late capitalism generates a banal conformity that the propaganda chiefs of Stalinism could only ever have dreamt of imposing. Zer0 Books knows that another kind of discourse – intellectual without being academic, popular without being populist – is not only possible: it is already flourishing, in the regions beyond the striplit malls of so-called mass media and the neurotically bureaucratic halls of the academy. Zer0 is committed to the idea of publishing as a making public of the intellectual. It is convinced that in the unthinking, blandly consensual culture in which we live, critical and engaged theoretical reflection is more important than ever before.